Cane, Rush and Straw

EXCALIBUR BOOKS

Edited by Yvonne Deutch

Published in the United States by
Excalibur Books
201 Park Avenue South
New York, New York 10003

© Marshall Cavendish Limited 1975, 1976, 1977

First printing 1977

Printed in Great Britain

ISBN 0-525-70068-4

This publication is not to be sold outside of
the U.S.A, Philippine Republic and Canada.

*Above: Straw weaving is one of
the most popular country crafts.
Many people make their own
corn dollies nowadays, and this
selection gives an idea of the
variety of shapes and patterns.*

Introduction

As our environment becomes more pressurized, many people are bringing the soothing products of country crafts into their homes. Scrubbed pine furniture, handwoven fabrics, baskets and mats made from cane and rush – even a tiny corn dolly presiding over the household – all these are ways of integrating town and country life-styles. More important still, there is a great revival of interest in learning the techniques of these old rustic skills, so that we do not have to depend on commercial products to get back to the roots of our crafts heritage.

Cane, Rush and Straw introduces you to the world of basketry, rush work and the ancient art of straw weaving. The beginner is taken step-by-step through various projects, starting from the basic stages, and progressing right through to more complicated weaves and shapes. Clear, concise instructions and practical working diagrams, as well as lavish photographs, all help you to achieve satisfying results from beautiful materials. Although you can buy ready prepared cane, rush and straw, you can also use flowers such as iris and montbretia from the hedgerow or garden. Perhaps you even know a river or pond where there are rushes growing.

You'll be delighted with the range of projects too, there are baskets in rush and cane for shopping and picnics, table mats, wine baskets – even pretty rush hats. You can also learn how to weave chair seats in cane and rush, or you may want to try an elegant bedhead. Everyone loves corn dollies, give them as gifts. Once you've started, you'll experience the pleasure of working creatively, and being in touch with a more relaxed way of living.

Contents

Cane

Basketry for today

Basketry is one of the oldest crafts known to humanity, and has been used all over the world for a variety of purposes. If we look around our own environment, it is fascinating to see the ways in which these ancient skills are applied. Next time you see a trendy young mother toting her bouncing offspring in a modern Moses basket, remember that she is carrying on a tradition of baby transport which was used by women long before the original Moses was stowed away in the bull rushes on the banks of the Nile. Despite the advances of technology, and the invention of synthetic materials, modern household fashion has revived interest in natural products, created from the most traditional and rustic skills, rather than the assembly line. The most attractive households today are more likely to reflect the atmosphere of the country cottage. This trend has been inspired by ordinary folk rather than designers – it seems that on the whole people prefer the appearance, texture and colour of a shopping basket in rush or cane to one made in imitation leather or plastic. Even the claims that synthetic products last longer, and are therefore more practical are not strong enough to affect this trend. In fact, anything made in cane or rush which is cared for properly will give years of service. What is most remarkable is that the instinct to bring back the products of country crafts to the home has given a whole new dimension to interior decoration. The sheer elegance of cane chairs, the harmony of rush matting, and the subtle detail of woven baskets, all combine to create a relaxed atmosphere which is vital in an era of high speed living. Even in many urban homes, a pretty corn dolly can often be found presiding over the family, a perfect symbol of the spirit of the countryside and the harvest coming together with the life of the big city. In adjusting the balance between past and present, we are discovering long lost pleasures in learning the skills of crafts such as basketry. Not only are there the obvious satisfactions derived from finding a new pastime or hobby, but also there is the sheer joy of working creatively with beautiful materials. The end results are unique craft products, with glowing textures, which add a truly human dimension to our lives.

Beginning with basketry

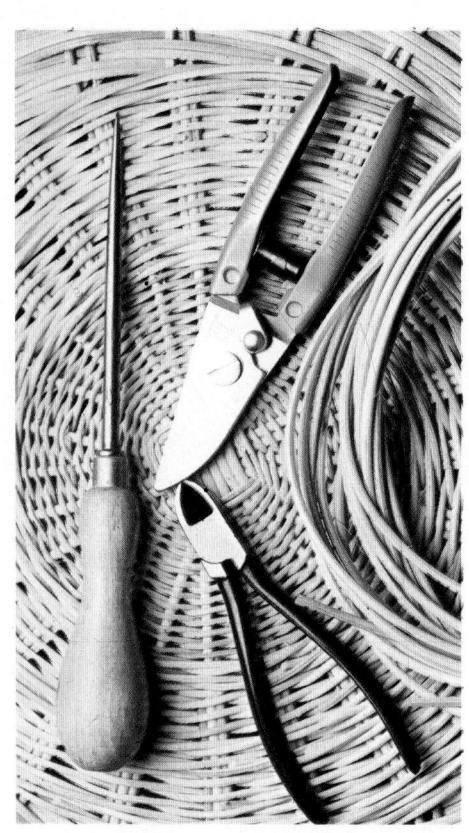

Above: Common tools and materials used in basketry are cane, basket maker's bodkin, secateurs (top) and side cutters (bottom).

Cane comes from the rattan family which is a creeper from SE Asia. It grows to enormous lengths and has sharp barbs. The outer layer is peeled off and discarded, while the bark is used for chair seating and handle wrapping. The inside pith or pulp is milled into canes of many thicknesses, from 000 (1mm) to 16 (5mm), and handle cane of 8mm or 10mm.

There are various qualities (all natural coloured, of course), 'blue tie' being the best, 'red' or 'green tie' and finally 'white tie' or bleached cane, which is rather poor in quality. Seagrass, strawplait, raffia, enamelled cane or wrapping cane can all be used to add colour and interest; cane can also be dyed with fabric dye.

Preparation

Cane must be soaked in hot water for about 30 minutes before using. Once you start you will soon be able to gauge the soaking time. If it dries while you are working just re-soak it until it is easy to handle. When you stop allow the work, plus all remaining cane, to dry before you put it away. Do not put damp cane into plastic bags as it will go mouldy.

Tools

The tools and equipment needed are inexpensive; some can be home-made and some improvised.

Side cutters, obtainable from tool shops, are useful but strong scissors, such as those used for flower arranging, or even garden secateurs will do.

A basket maker's bodkin is essential It is used to form channels for canes to thread into or to split the cane. You can buy one from a craft supplier or improvise with an old, sharpened screwdriver or a medium-sized knitting needle.

Tape measure

Clothes pegs [pins] are useful for holding the work in place.

Techniques

There are various ways to begin a basket. Initially you can use a plastic or wooden base with holes in it made specially for basket making. You can use any base to suit your requirements as long as it has an odd number of holes. However, as these bases limit the design potential, only use them in order to become familiar with the materials. The holes in the base are not always big enough to hold thick cane which means that you cannot make a large, sturdy basket. Bases also tend to make a basket heavy. However, the picnic basket will teach you the basic techniques.

These baskets are made using a plywood or laminated plastic base. the larger one is ideal for picnics, and the smaller one is suitable for a child.

The picnic basket

This strong basket will give you years of use. It is designed to hold two flasks and a sandwich box in the middle.

Prepare the cane by soaking it in hot water for 30 minutes.

For the ribs ie the upright stakes; cut 49 stakes of No.8 (3mm) cane 52cm (20in) long. Insert one stake into each hole allowing 10cm (4in) to protrude on the wrong side of the base. If the cane is difficult to push through the holes you can widen them with the bodkin. Alternatively, as the cane swells when wet, insert the canes before soaking and soak them afterwards.

To make a foot border under the basket, hold the base with the right side towards you and the short stake ends away from you. Starting with any stake end, bend it down to the right behind the next stake and back to the front. Then pass it in front of the next two stakes and tuck it to the back through the next space (fig.1).

Repeat with each stake in turn. It will help if you say to yourself "Behind one, in front of two, and tuck it in". At the end of the round weave the stakes in and out of stakes that have already been turned down. You may have to push these stakes up a bit to get the others through. When they are all in place, give each stake a little pull to see that they are all tight and level. Place the basket right side up on the table. Put some sort of weight (a stone, flat iron) inside the basket to keep it steady. This will make it easier to hold the work and also to keep the shape you want.

Now you have to wale Waling is a weave used for strength and is put on the bottom and the top of a basket. When a basket starts to lose its shape, a band of waling will help to retain it. It can be done with three, four, five or six weavers – use three weavers here.

Insert three lengths of No.5 (2.5mm) cane, to be used as weavers, into any three consecutive spaces. Mark the stake immediately to the left of the first one in some way. Take the left hand weaver to the right in front of two stakes, over the top of the other two weavers and around the back of the next stake to the front again (fig.2). Now use the next left hand weaver and do exactly the same as before and then repeat with each weaver in turn all the way around the basket and back to the marked stake (fig.3).

Here you have to do a 'step-up' If you don't, the work jumps up and spirals and the weave doesn't have the continuous rope effect that it should. You have to do this step-up at this spot on every round and then continue as you started.

Take the right hand weaver in front of two, behind one and through to the front again (fig.4). Take the middle one in front of two and behind one. Take the left one in front of two and behind one (fig.5). All the weavers should now come out of the same three

---

Picnic basket

You will need :
227g (½lb) No.8 (3mm) cane.
113g (¼lb) No.5 (2.5mm) cane.
3m (3yd) 10mm handle cane.
5.5m (6yd) glossy wrapping cane or 7.5m (8yd) No.6 (2.6mm) chair seating cane.
1m (1yd) enamelled cane – optional.
56g (2oz) sea-grass – optional.
Oblong plywood or plastic base 15cm by 41cm (6in by 16in) with 49 holes.
Side-cutters – you can use garden secateurs instead.
A bodkin – you can use a medium size knitting needle instead.

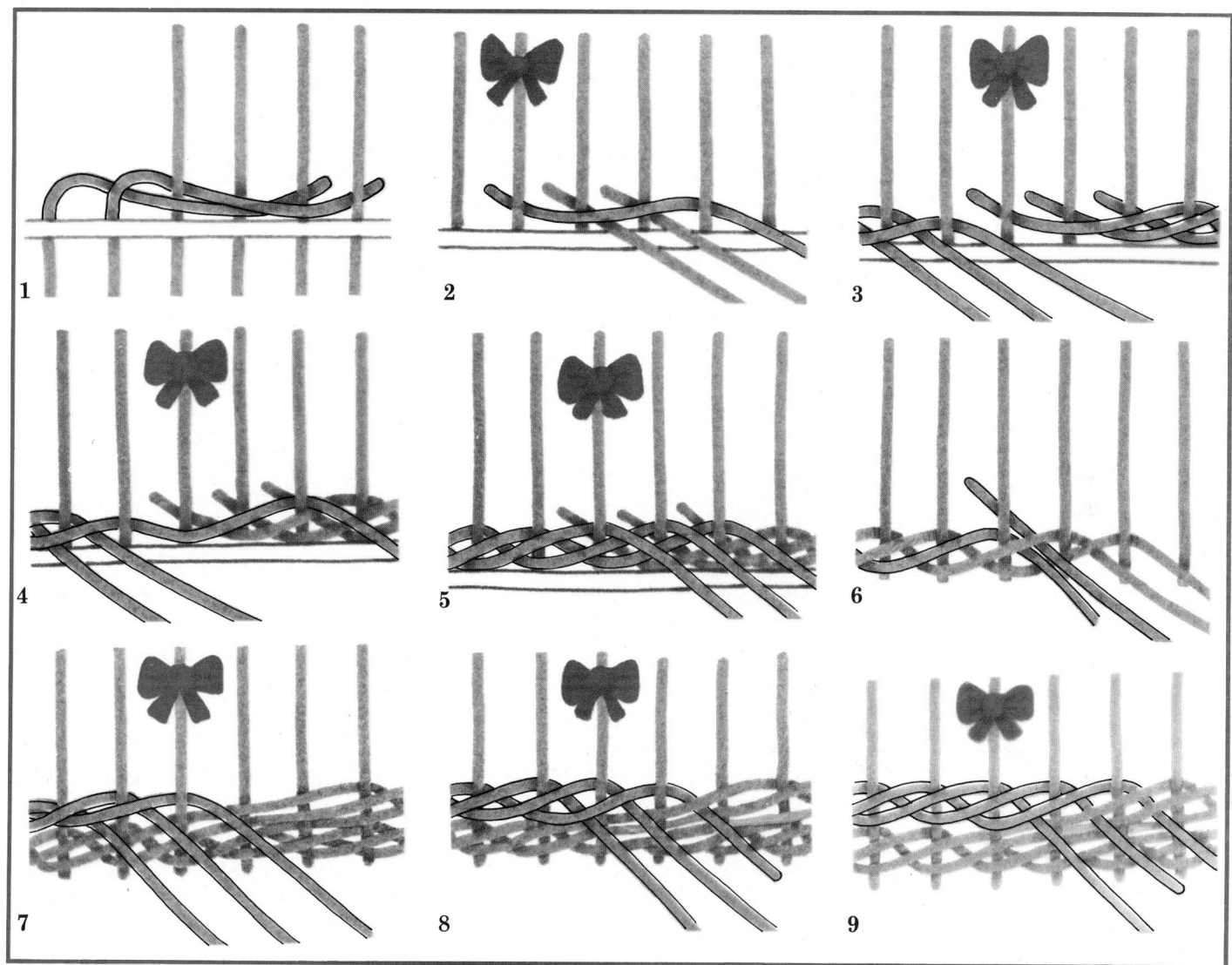

spaces you started with. Continue until you reach the marked stake again and step-up. Put on five rounds of waling, remembering to step-up at the marked stake, joining in new lengths when necessary. Now you are ready to join in the weavers.

Joining weavers Join in when the cane which has run out is on the left of the other weavers. Pull it backwards slightly and insert the new cane into the hole beside, and to the right of, the old one. This means that the old and new weavers will lie side by side and the old end will be to the front and the new end will be inside the basket (fig.6). The ends are neatened later.

To complete the five rounds of waling use the left hand weaver (not

1. The foot border.
2. The start of waling.
3. Starting the step-up.
4. First stage of step-up.
5. The step-up completed.
6. Joining new cane in waling.
7. The end of the waling.
8. Next stage in finishing waling.
9. Completed waling before trimming the ends.

10

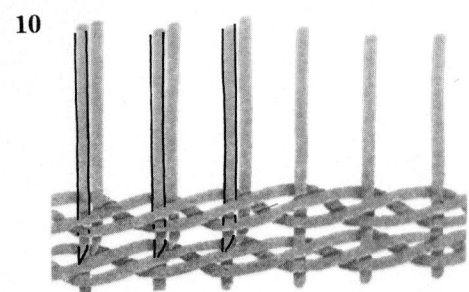

11

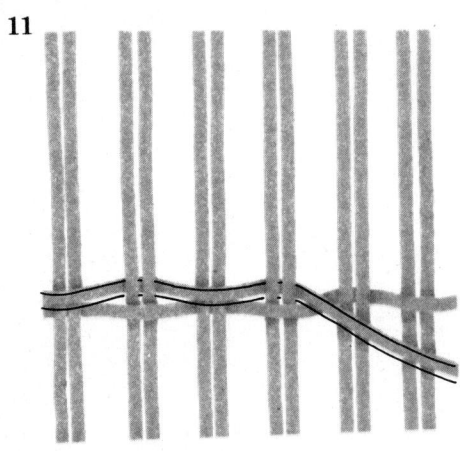

12a

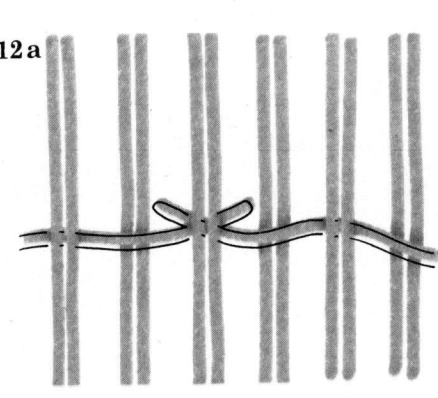

12b

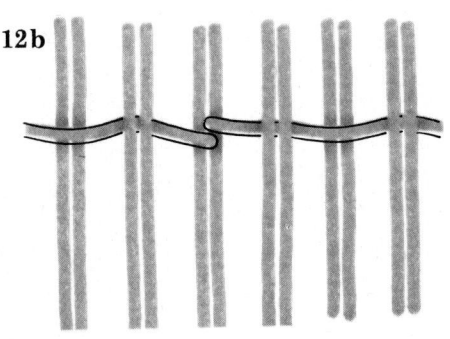

the right one this time), in front of two, behind one and to the front again. This will go round the back of the marked stake. Cut it off to about 8cm (3in) (fig.7). Now use the next left hand weaver and pass it in front of two, behind one and through to the front, but on its way to the front thread it under the top cane of the previous round. Cut this one off (fig.8). Use the last weaver now, in front of two and behind one, but thread it under the top two canes of the previous round, and cut it off (fig.9).

Bye-stakes are extra stakes that lie beside the main stakes to make the basket stronger. Cut one bye-stake for each stake, 41cm (16in) long of No.8 (3mm) cane. Make a point at one end of each and insert them into the waling, one on the right of each stake. They must lie in the same channel as the main stake. Use the bodkin to help form a passage for them to slip into (fig.10).

Randing is a weave for economy and speed. It is very easy and only one weaver is used at a time. Put a weaver of No.5 (2.5mm) cane into any space and weave to the right, in front of one pair and behind one pair. Continue all the way round. There is no step-up in randing (fig.11) because you are only using one weaver.

Shaping You must concentrate on the shaping. Every time a weaver goes around the front of a stake, hold that stake with the thumb and forefinger of the left hand. As you want the sides of the basket to go up straight you must hold the stake upright.

To join in a new weaver leave the old one at the back of a stake and place the new one against the same stake at the back (fig.12a). Leave the ends until the siding is finished and then trim off with a slanting cut so that they won't catch on anything in the basket (fig.12b). Use the side cutters to trim off.

Rand for 9cm (3½in) keeping the sides quite straight. Wale for three rounds with No.5 (2.5mm) cane and step-up as before.

Preparing for the handles At this point start making room for the handles to fit into later. Cut four pieces of the handle cane about 23cm (9in) long, for liners, and slype one end.

Slyping is a special way to cut cane to a point. It is done by making cuts on two consecutive quarters of the cane (fig.13). Slypes can be any length but start these 5cm (2in) from the end.

Insert four 'handle liners' into the siding of the basket, beside four stakes and where you want your handle to be. Allow eight stakes between the two liners on each side. Continue to weave around stake and liner together to form holes for the real handle.

Rand for 2.5cm (1in) with sea-grass. You could substitute flat cane, raffia or No.5 (2.5mm) cane. Wale for three rounds with No.5 (2.5mm) cane. Rand for 2.5cm (1in) with sea-grass. Wale for three rounds with No.5 (2.5mm) cane.

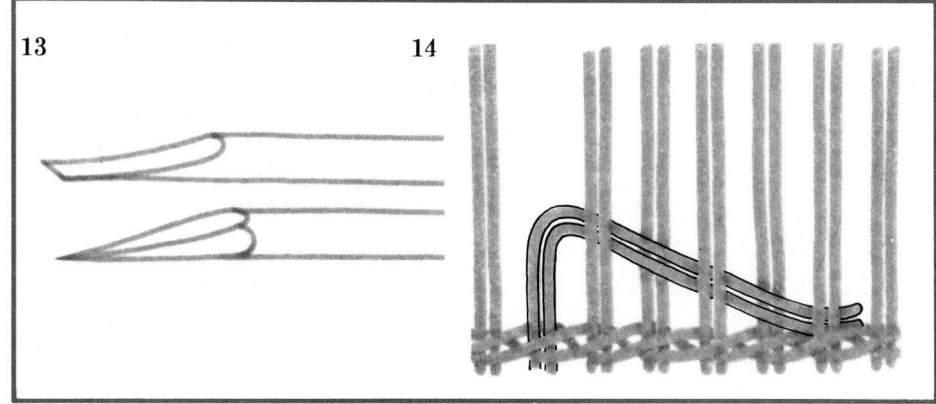

The illustrations opposite
continue the stages of making
the foot border.
10. Inserting bye-stakes.
11. Randing.
12a. Front view of new cane being
joined in randing.
12b. Back view of join with the
ends trimmed back.
13. A slype made with two cuts.
14. Starting a trac border.

Trac border The sides of this basket are finished with a trac border. Re-soak the stakes if necessary and start with any stake and refer to it as the first and the next one to the right as second, and so on. Bend the first stake and bye-stake together, 4cm (1½in) up from the waling, with quite a sharp bend. Pass this pair behind the second pair, in front of the third, behind the fourth, in front of the fifth and tuck them to the inside behind the sixth pair (fig.14).

Now bend the second pair down, making sure that the elbow of the bend is exactly the same height as the first bend. Repeat the weaving as for the previous pair and tuck them in behind the seventh pair.

Repeat with each pair in turn and finish in exactly the same way, although you will weave the last few in front and behind stakes that have already been turned down. Be sure to keep them all in the correct order and don't let any cross over any others. Go in front of and behind the handle liners, together with the adjacent stake, and keep the pattern correct. Trim all ends of the weavers and the stakes with a diagonal cut so that they do not stick out. The border stake ends must lie against a stake or they will slip to the front.

Cut two pieces of prepared handle cane each 65cm (26in) long and slype all the ends. Bend into U-shapes. Remove the handle liners and keep them as they can be used again. Insert the handles well down into the spaces so the weaving grips them tightly. The handles should be about 13cm (5in) high.

Insert a length of prepared wrapping cane, wrong side uppermost, into the siding, just under the border and to the immediate right of one of the handles. It should protrude 15cm (6in) to the inside (fig.15). Bring this short, protruding end up and over the top of the border, then down and across in front of the handle and the border. Re-insert it into the siding again just under the border, but this time to the left of the handle. Bring this same end up to lie behind the handle where it will be bound later.

Below: Starting to wrap the handle with the wrapping cane in position.

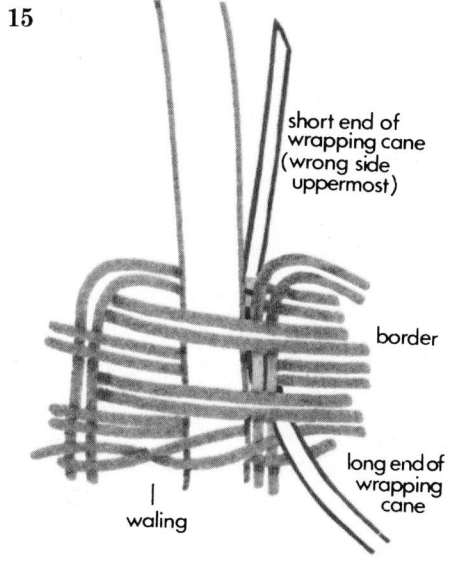

15

short end of wrapping cane (wrong side uppermost)

border

long end of wrapping cane

waling

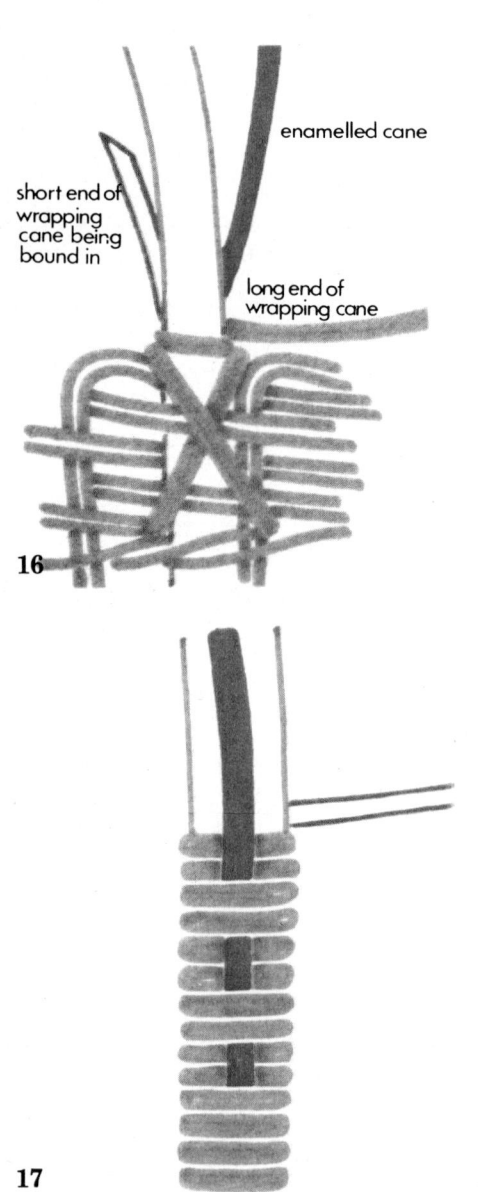

enamelled cane

short end of
wrapping
cane being
bound in

long end of
wrapping cane

16

17

Top: Wrapping the handle.
Above: Side view of handle
wrapping showing the weaving
over and under the
enamelled cane.

Cut a piece of enamelled cane (or wrapping cane), 41cm (16in) long, and insert it into the siding so that it lies against the outer curve of the handle, right side out. Use a peg to keep it in place temporarily (fig.16). Take the long end of the wrapping cane up and across the handle and the border so that a cross is formed in front of the border. Wrap this along and around the handle four times, binding in both the short end and the enamelled cane. Continue to wrap the handle tightly but pass it over and under the enamelled cane to form a pattern (fig.17). This is not only decorative but helps to keep the wrapping tight. This handle was wrapped under twice and over twice but you can make any pattern you like.

Continue wrapping handle, keeping the enamelled cane at the top and finish as you began with four plain wraps and a cross in front of the border to match the other end. Weave the end in and out of the waling to secure it firmly and neatly.

If you need to join in a new piece of cane lay the new cane, wrong side out, underneath the handle, when there is still enough of the old wrapping left to do another 5cm (2in). Continue to wrap with the old cane, binding the new cane in, until there is only 4cm (1½in) left of the old piece. Turn the new piece so that the right side is on the outside and commence wrapping with it. At the same time lay the old piece on the underside of the handle and bind it in with the wrapping. This makes an invisible join.

The handles need to be secured with a peg so that they will not slip out from the basket. While the handle cane is still wet, pierce it with a bodkin between the first and second rounds of the top waling. To make the peg point a short piece of No.10 (3.35mm) cane, or a wedge of the handle cane, and insert it into the hole made by the bodkin. It must come right through to the inside. You may have to tap it in with a hammer. Cut this peg off, on the inside and the outside of the basket, level with the waling. This forms a peg which prevents the handles from slipping out. Repeat on the other three places where the handles enter the sides.

Finish the basket by shaping the handles. Make them curve towards each other by tying them together at the top while they are still wet. At the same time keep the sides of the basket apart by placing a book or a block of wood inside at border level. Leave it in position until the handles are dry.

General hints

Although the picnic basket represents something of a trial run in the basic techniques, you have still put a lot of effort into the work, so remember to care for it properly. It is sturdy, but not indestructible. If it does get wet, dry it with a cloth.

Round mats and bases

The inside or centre of a table mat is the beginning of most baskets, regardless of size or shape. To become familiar with the making of the centre – ie a woven base – and the technique of pairing, make these mats in various sizes. At the same time you will be using the techniques of waling and making a trac border learned in the previous chapter on the picnic basket.

Table mats

Cane place mats look handsome on any table – they're good insulators and they thrive on being scrubbed clean with water – not soap. And you'll be thrilled at the cost. The quantities given are enough to make six mats of 19cm (7½in) diameter or four mats of 24cm (9½in) or ten mats of 12.5cm (5in) diameter.

The 19cm (7½in) mat

Cut eight pieces of No.8 (3mm) cane 17cm (6½in) long. These are for the base sticks which form the spokes of the mat. Point four of them at one end, and make a split of about 2.5cm (1in) in the centre of the other four. Use the bodkin to form the split. Thread all four of the pointed sticks into the split sticks so that they form a cross (fig.1). Bend a length of prepared (ie soaked in hot water for about 30 minutes) No.3 (2mm) cane roughly in the middle. Make this bend quite sharp. If the cane will not bend without cracking, twist it with the thumbs and forefingers of both hands held closely together. Twist each hand in opposite directions until the fibres of the cane give way. Loop this bend around one 'arm' of the cross and bring both ends to the front (fig.2). These two ends of cane form two weavers and will now be referred to as the left-hand weaver and the right-hand weaver in the following instructions.

Pairing Take the left-hand weaver in front of the same arm, over the top of the other weaver, around the back of the next arm and then to the front again as shown in fig.3. Repeat with the other end: across in front of one arm, over the other weaver and around the back of the next arm (fig.3). The diagram is overleaf. This is called pairing and is nearly always used for round and oval

Table mats
You will need : 170g (6oz) No.5 (2.5mm) cane. 113g (4oz) No.3 (2mm) cane. 283g (10oz) No.8 (3mm) cane. Side-cutters. Bodkin.

Below: The base of the mat is formed by a cross made of two sets of sticks.
Bottom: First steps in pairing.

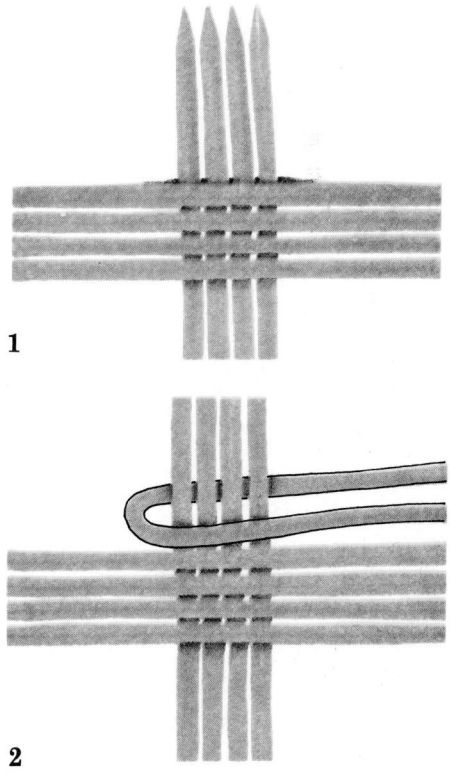

1

2

15

bases. Basically it's 'in front of one and behind one' and you should turn the work around with each stroke. Continue in this way until you have gone right around twice.

On the third round the arms must be opened into pairs. Instead of going right around the back of each arm, on the second part of the stroke bring the weaver to the front in between the middle two, making two pairs (fig.4). Repeat all the way round so that you have eight pairs evenly spaced (fig.5).

Weave in the same way for another two rounds, making five rounds in all, then open all the sticks on the next round so that they are all single (fig.6) and form into spokes.

Joining If you need to join a new piece of cane, wait until the old one is on the outside. Pull it back with your left thumb and slip the new cane into the work so that it lies between this end and the work. The old end will protrude to the front and the new one to the back (fig.7). The diagram is shown overleaf.

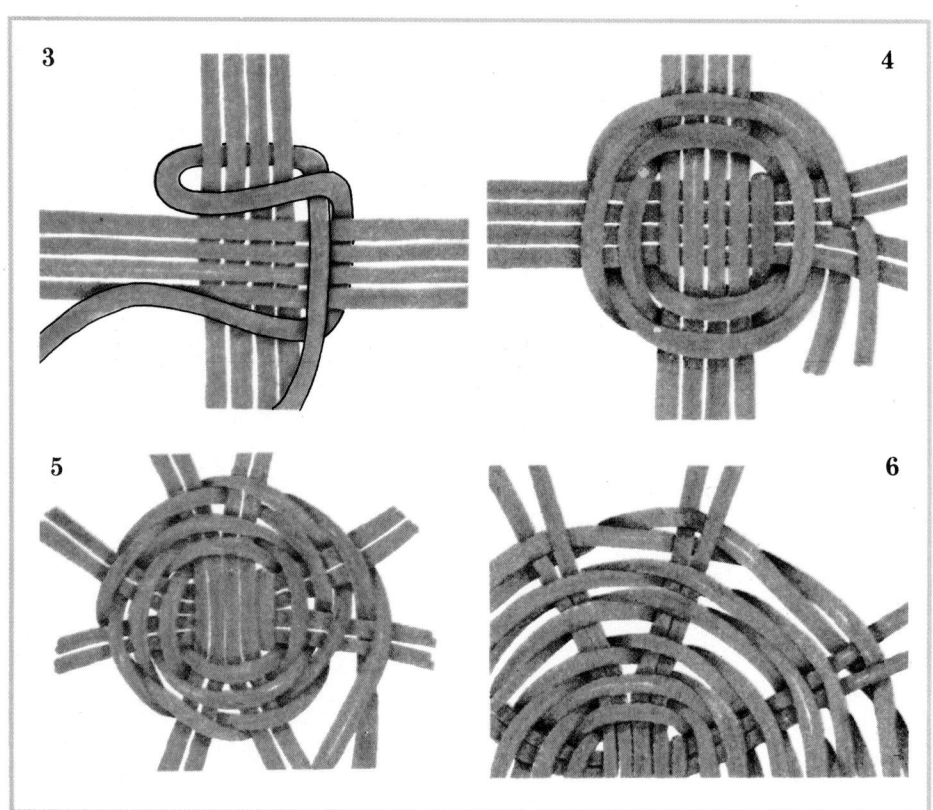

3. Pairing continued.
4. On the third round, cross is opened to form the spokes.
5. The cross opened to form eight pairs.
6. Pairs opened to single spokes.

Continue to pair until the work has a diameter of 9cm (3½in). Secure the pairing by threading the weavers under one cane of the previous round. Try to do this as invisibly as possible.

Join in three weavers of No.3 (2mm) cane. This can be done in two ways: a) they can be laid in three consecutive spaces or b) they can be inserted into the weaving down by the side of three consecutive sticks and then bent down to the front (fig.8). If you use method a) clip the ends down with a clothes peg until you have woven over them (fig.9). The diagram is shown on the opposite page.

Put on three rounds of waling with these three weavers. Step up after each round and finish off ends. Pair for four rounds. Wale for another two rounds. Trim all the ends of the weavers close to the work and cut off any surplus stick ends protruding.

To make a trac border Cut 32 border stakes of No.5 (2.5mm) cane 30cm (12in) long. Soak them in hot water for 10 minutes. Point one end of each stake. Insert one stake into the weaving on both sides of every stick. Insert the pointed ends and push them right down as far as they will go. Use the bodkin to form a channel for the stakes to slip into the correct position.

Put on a trac border. Bend each pair of border stakes in turn down to the right about 2.5cm (1in) beyond the waling. Pass them behind the next pair, in front of the next, then behind and in front again. Tuck them into the back of the work in the next space. Repeat all the way around. The last few pairs will weave in and out of stakes that are already bent down. Secure them firmly.

Trim the ends of the stakes with a diagonal cut so that the ends lie snugly and safely against a stake. Do not cut them too short or the ends will slip through to the front; if they are too long they will catch onto things and make the mat unstable.

The 24cm (9½in) mat

You will need the same materials as before. The same quantity of cane will make four mats of this size. The instructions are similar to the previous ones but the measurements and numbers differ slightly because of the different size.

Cut ten pieces of No.8 (3mm) cane 20cm (8in) long. Split five of these in the centre with the bodkin and point the other five at one end. Thread the pointed pieces through the split to form a cross.

Using prepared No.3 (2mm) cane, pair for two rounds. On the third round open the arms in two pairs with an odd one in the middle. Each arm will now be split into 2,1,2, (fig.10).

Pair for three rounds and then open the sticks into singles. Continue pairing until the work measures 11cm (4½in) in diameter. Put on two rounds of waling, five rounds of pairing and then a

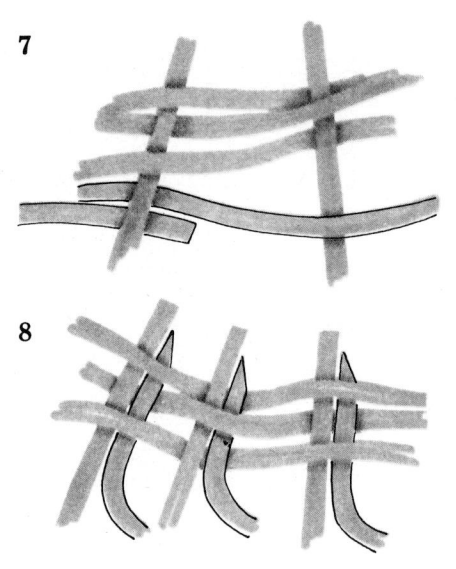

7

8

Top: Joining in a new piece of cane.
Above: Inserting cane for waling.

further two rounds of waling. Trim the ends of the weavers and cut off any surplus sticks protruding beyond the waling.

Cut 40 pieces of prepared No.5 (2.5mm) cane 30cm (12in) long. Point one end of each piece and insert this end into the weaving of the base, one each side of each stick. Put on a trac border and trim all the surplus ends off with your side cutters.

The 12.5cm (5in) mat

The same quantity of materials as before will make ten small mats. Cut six base sticks of No.8 (3mm) cane 15cm (6in) long and thread three pointed ones into three split ones to make a cross (see fig. 1). Pair for two rounds with No.3 (2mm) cane.

Open all the sticks to singles on the third round and continue to pair until the work measures 6cm (2½in). Wale for two rounds. Trim weavers and sticks. Cut 24 border stakes of No.5 (2.5mm) cane and put on a trac border, finishing as before.

The cheese platter

For a cheese platter 38cm (15in) in diameter thicker cane is used, as the larger a piece of work is, the thicker and stronger the cane must be. The techniques are similar to those used for making the smaller mats. The cheese platter is simply a larger version.

Start with 12 base sticks of No.10 cane 31cm (12½in) long. Soak them for about 20 minutes. Pierce six in the centre and point one end of the other six. Thread the pointed ones through splits to form a flat cross. If the sticks bunch together make the splits larger so that they remain flat. Bend a length of prepared No.5 (2.5mm) cane in the centre and loop it around one arm of the cross.

Pair for two rounds, keeping the sticks of each arm together. On the third round open the sticks into 12 groups of pairs, evenly all around the base. Put on four more rounds of pairing then open the sticks into singles. Continue pairing until the work measures 14cm (5½in) in diameter. Join in new lengths of prepared cane as needed. Wale for two rounds, pair for four rounds, wale for two rounds, pair for four rounds, wale for two rounds. Trim all the surplus ends of the weavers and sticks with the side cutters.

Cut 48 pieces of No.8 (3mm) cane 52cm (20in) long. Point one end of each piece. Insert them into the weaving of the base, one on each side of each base stick. Insert them as far as the waling nearest to the centre to make a distinctive pattern.

Put on a trac border. Bend a pair down to the right 4.5cm (1¾in) beyond the waling. Weave this pair behind and then in front of the next stakes three times, and then tuck it to the back in the next space. Repeat with each pair of stakes in turn. The last few will

9

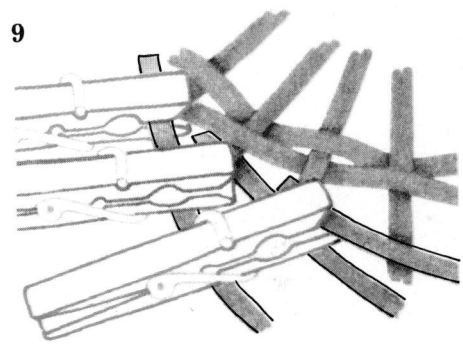

10

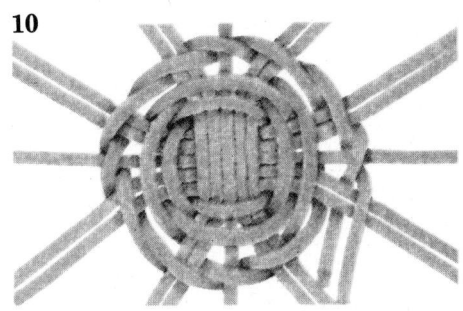

Top: Using clothes pegs [pins] to hold the cane.
Above: Opening the cross to form the spokes.

Cheese platter
You will need :   56g (2oz) No.10 (3.35mm) cane.   56g (2oz) No.5 (2.5mm) cane.   56g (2oz) No.8 (3mm) cane.   Side-cutters.   Bodkin.

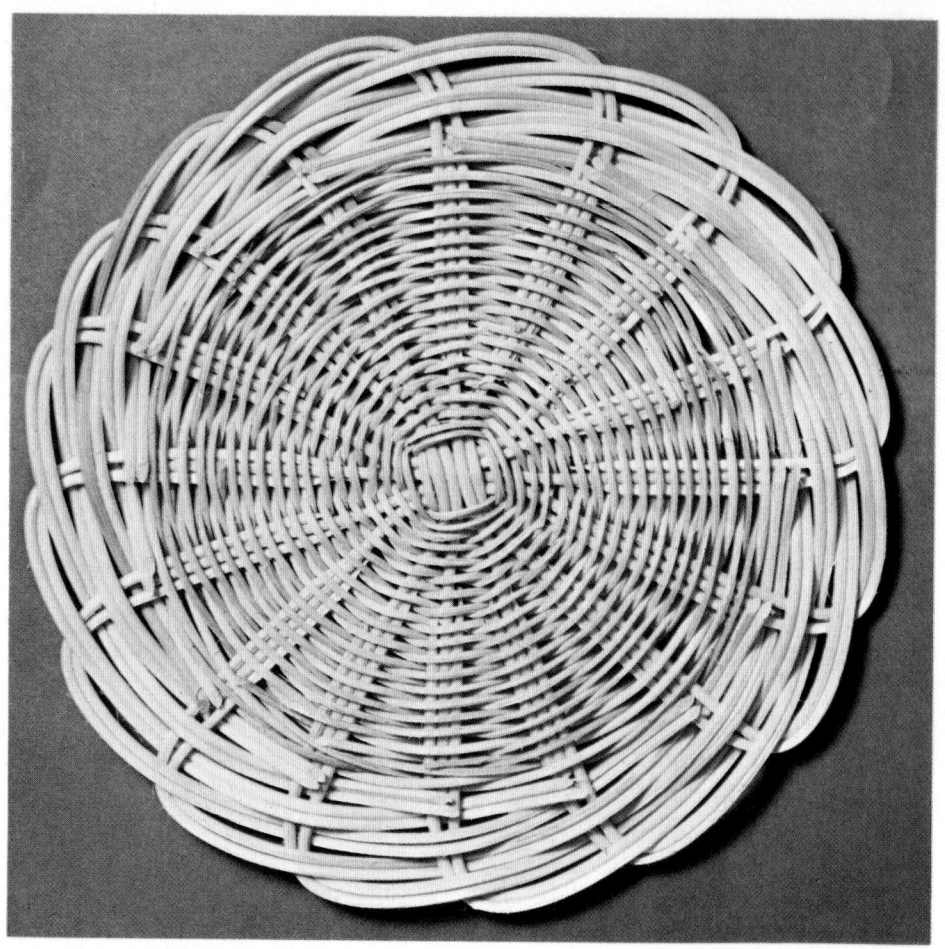

Right: The wrong side of the mat shows the end of the cane lying against the spokes. The cane must not be cut too short or the ends will slip to the front. Opposite: A set of platters with sloping sides and decorative borders.

weave behind and in front of stakes that are already bent down. Make sure that each pair is bent down exactly the same distance from the weaving and that work is even. Trim the ends of the stakes diagonally so that the ends lie snugly and safely against a stake.

General hints

To help you to make a neat, closely woven base follow these hints: Make quite sure that the left weaver passes over the top of the other one on its way to the back.

Never leave one of the weavers at the back of the work – it must return to the front before you use the next one.

If you hold the base too tightly in your left hand it will curl up towards you. Try to hold it loosely and, in this case, flat.

If you find that the rounds of weaving have a gap between them, try pulling each weaver down hard when it is at the back of the work and then merely slip it to the front.

Making
shaped platters

Basketry designs are endless and once you have mastered the basic weaving techniques it is possible to make any number of articles without ever repeating the same design.

Basketry techniques can be used to make a variety of objects. The baskets illustrated here can be used in different ways and are easy to make. They make eye-catching party dishes for chips, nuts and canapés or you can use them as platters to hold flat oven dishes. If you are really ambitious you can join them together to make a tiered stand for a festive floral arrangement which is also sturdy enough to be heaped with fruit and nuts.

Flat baskets

Instructions are for three baskets with diameters of 18cm (7in), 25cm (10in) and 35cm (14in) which can be made into a stand. Prepare, ie soak, the cane before starting the baskets.

The 25cm (10in) basket

Use No.10 (3.35mm), No.3 (2mm), No.4 (2.25mm) and No.5 (2.5mm) cane which has been soaked well.

Cut eight base sticks of No.10 (3.35mm) cane 20cm (8in) long. Make a point at one end of four of the pieces. Using the bodkin split the other four in the centre and insert the pointed sticks into the split to form a cross. If the sticks bunch up then the splits are not long enough, so make sure your slits are properly made.

Flat baskets
You will need : 56g (2oz) No.10 (3.35mm) cane. 113g (4oz) No.4 (2.25mm) cane. 170g (6oz) No.5 (2.5mm) cane. 113g (4oz) No.8 (3mm) cane. 56g (2oz) No.12 (3.75mm) cane. 113g (4oz) No.3 (2mm) cane. 113g (4oz) No.13 (4mm) cane (for tiered stand only). Side-cutters. Bodkin.

Right: Additional stakes are added to the base for putting on the border.

1

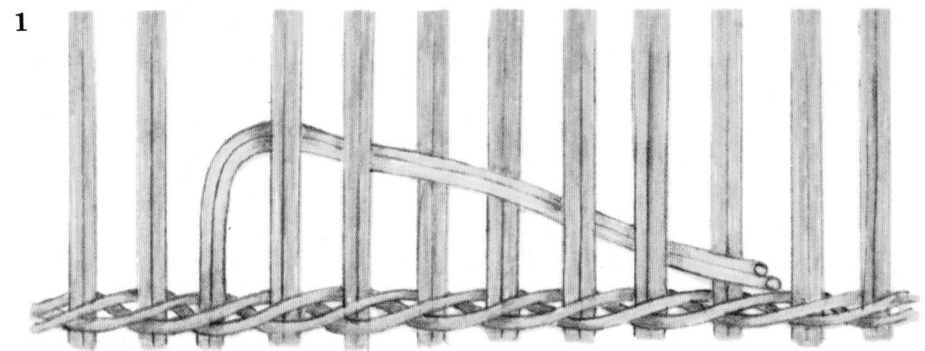

Left: *Starting the border: bend the sides up and inwards to complete the shape.*

Bend a length of prepared No.3 (2mm) cane – not quite centrally or the two ends will then be used up at the same time. To bend the cane break the fibres by twisting them with the fingers. Loop the cane where you have bent it over one 'arm' of the cross and bring both ends down to the front to form two weavers.

Pair for two rounds keeping all the sticks of each arm together. On the third round open the arms of the cross into pairs. Don't expect the weaving to open the sticks. You have to pull the sticks apart with your fingers to get the correct shape. Continue to pair for four more rounds, when you have to open them out.

Open the sticks so that they are all single like the spokes of a wheel. Continue pairing until the work has a diameter of 15cm (6in), joining in new weavers when necessary. Insert three lengths of No.4 (2.25mm) cane into any three consecutive spaces. Mark the stick immediately to the left of the left hand weaver. Wale for three rounds. Remember to do a step-up each time you reach the marked stick. Complete the three rounds of waling up to the marked stick. Then take the left hand weaver in front of two sticks and behind the marked stick and back to the front. Take the next weaver on the left in front of two sticks, behind one but thread it under the top weaver of the previous round on its way to the front.

Repeat with the last weaver but thread it under the top weavers of the previous rounds on its way to front. Trim all surplus ends of sticks, using your side cutters.

Cut 64 stakes of No.5 (2.5mm) cane 30cm (12in) long and point one end of each stake. Insert the pointed ends of the stakes into the work. Insert two stakes on each side of each base stick. Insert two weavers of No.3 (2mm) cane into the base weaving and pair for four rounds keeping the stakes in pairs.

To shape the bowl wale for another three rounds but as you work gradually push the stakes up and away from you and weave in this position keeping the stakes in pairs. Remember to step-up on each round when waling. Finish as before.

Right: Platters can be stacked on top of each other to form a tiered fruit stand.

The border Starting with any pair of stakes bend them down to the right about 4cm (1½in) from the waling. Pass them behind the next two pairs, in front of the next two pairs, behind two pairs and back to the front which is the underside of the bowl (fig.1). While you are making the border try to bend the sides up and away from you to complete the bowl shape.

Repeat with each pair of stakes in turn. The last few stakes will pass in front and behind stakes that are already turned down. Keep the pattern correct and the stakes in their correct position. When you are finished you should not be able to see where you started and where you finished. Trim all surplus ends. Be careful not to cut border stake ends too short or they will slip through to the inside.

The 18cm (7in) basket

Use No.8 (3mm), No.3 (2mm), No.5 (2.5mm) and No.4 (2.25mm) cane which has been soaked for 30 minutes.

Cut six base sticks of No.8 (3mm) cane 13cm (5in) long. Pierce three in the centre and split them. Point one end of the other three and insert them into three split sticks to form a cross.

Bend a length of prepared No.3 (2mm) cane and pair for two rounds before opening the sticks singly. Continue to pair until the work measures 9cm (3½in) across. Wale for two rounds stepping up on the first round and finishing as before on the second round. Trim. Cut 48 stakes of No.5 (2.5mm) cane 25cm (10in) long. Point one end of each stake and insert the pointed ends into the work – two on each side of each base stick. Insert two weavers of No.4 (2.25mm) cane and pair for three rounds keeping the pairs together. Insert three lengths of No.4 (2.25mm) cane and wale for two rounds shaping the bowl as before. Complete the bowl by putting on the same border as before and shaping the basket as you work.

The 35cm (14in) basket

Use No.12 (3.75mm), No.4 (2.25mm), No.5 (2.5mm) and No.8 (3mm) cane which has been soaked for 30 minutes.

Cut 10 sticks of No.12 (3.75mm) cane 23cm (9in) long. Pierce five in the centre and point one end of the other five. Insert the pointed sticks into the split to form a cross. Pair for two rounds with No.4 (2.25cm) cane in the usual manner.

Open the arms of the cross out to the pattern of 2-1-2 on each arm. Pair like this for six rounds and then open out into single sticks. Continue to pair until the work measures 20cm (8in) across. Finish off the pairing and trim the ends of the weavers.

Insert three lengths of No.5 (2.5cm) cane and wale for three rounds stepping up on the first two rounds and finishing as before on the third round. You are now ready to insert the stakes.

Cut 80 stakes of No.8 (3mm) cane 35cm (14in) long and point one end of each. Insert the pointed end into the work – two on each side of each base stick – as before.

Insert two lengths of No.4 (2.25mm) cane. Keep the stakes double and pair for eight rounds bending the work up and away from you to shape the bowl and make an attractive curve.

Insert three lengths of No.5 (2.5mm) cane and wale for three rounds stepping up on the first two rounds and finishing on the third round. You are now ready to make a border.

Put on the same border as before but this time bend each pair of stakes 4.5cm (1¾in) from the waling. It is a bit more difficult to make this border as you are working with No.8 (3mm) cane. Soak the work well and keep shaping it as you work. Trim off the surplus ends, using your side cutters.

The tiered stand

If you have made the three baskets and want to stack them don't be worried because it looks difficult. The stand is 38cm (15in) high and made from No.13 (4mm) and No.5 (2.5mm) cane.

Cut ten stakes of No.13 (4mm) cane 52cm (20in) long and point one end of each piece. Soak well – at least 30 minutes in hot water. These stakes will pass through the three baskets and the ends will be used to make a border underneath the large basket with a similar one on the top and smallest basket.

Starting with the larger basket make ten holes 5cm (2in) from the centre. Use the bodkin to open the work so that you do not damage the cane. Space the holes evenly to form a circle with a diameter of 10cm (4in). Insert the stakes so that 8cm (3in) protrudes from the wrong side of the basket. Wale for two rounds on the underside of the basket with No.5 (2.5mm) cane.

The footing Using the short ends on the underside of the basket put on the foot border by bending each stake in turn, down to the right, in front of one and then tuck it behind the next so that it is on the inside of the ring (fig.2). The last stake will have to be passed under a stake which has already been turned down. Turn the work the right way up and pull each stake in turn until the footing rests evenly and securely on a flat surface.

Wale with No.5 (2.5mm) cane on top side of basket for four rounds on the stakes stepping up on the first three rounds and finishing on the fourth. You are now ready to insert bye-stakes.

Bye-stakes are inserted next to the stakes for additional strength. Cut ten bye-stakes of No.13 (4mm) cane 19cm (7½in) long and point one end of each. Be very accurate when measuring these as they

2

Above: Working the foot border.

level the next basket. Insert the pointed ends of the bye-stakes into the waling, one to the right of each stake. Put on one round of fitching 14cm (5½in) from the waling.

To fitch bend a piece of No.5 (2.5mm) cane roughly in the centre and loop it around a stake where the fitching is required. Let the two ends come to the front of the work to form two weavers. Grasp both weavers in the thumb and forefinger of the right hand and twist them towards you so that the right hand weaver comes over the top of the other. Slip the under one (or left one) round the back of the next stake and back to the front (fig.3). Repeat all the way around. Do not allow the circle of stakes to get wider while you are fitching. Keep the fitching level so that it is the same distance from the work all around.

Insert another No.5 (2.5mm) cane and wale for three rounds stepping up on the first two rounds and finishing off on the third round. Make quite sure that all the bye-stakes are the same height. Trim them if necessary so that they are level with the waling. *Be careful not to cut any of the long stakes.*

Use the bodkin and make ten holes in centre basket to form a circle around the centre with a diameter of 8cm (3in). Thread the ten stakes on the large basket through these holes and push the centre basket down onto the waling. Make sure that it is level. Put four rounds of waling with No.5 (2.5mm) cane onto the stakes. Step-up on the first three rounds and finish on the fourth round.

Cut ten bye-stakes of No.13 (4mm) cane 16.5cm (6½in) long, point one end of each and insert the pointed end to the right of each stake and into the waling. Fitch as before 11.5cm (4½in) away from the waling and then insert another No.5 (2.5mm) cane and wale for three rounds. Trim the bye-stakes so that they are level and flush with the waling, making sure that none of them protrude.

Make ten holes in the small basket to form a circle around the centre with a diameter of 5cm (2in). Thread the ten stakes through these holes and push the basket down level onto the waling. Wale for three rounds with No.5 (2.5mm) cane on the top of the small basket. Now you are ready to put on the border.

Use the stake ends to put on the same border as you did for the footing underneath the large basket. The tiered basket is complete when you have trimmed all the excess ends.

General hints

Whether you have decided to make the baskets separately, or stacked them together to make a tiered stand, you'll want to take care of them properly. Remember not to stuff them with heavy objects, dust them frequently, and give them an occasional scrub.

3

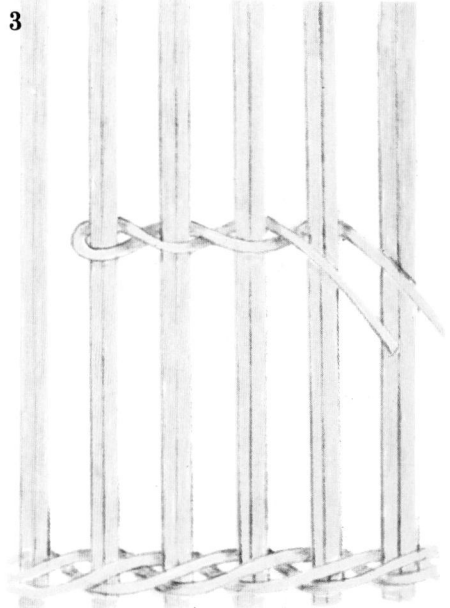

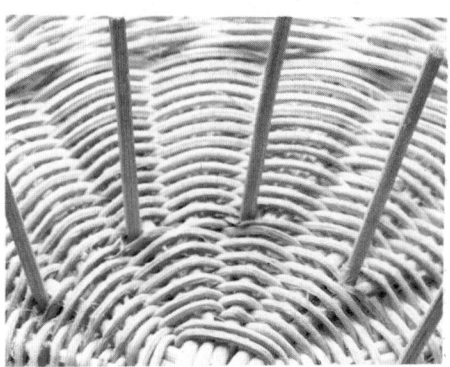

Top: Fitching: keep this level and same distance from work all around.
Above: Ends protruding from bottom of the large basket.

Two baskets

The instructions for these sturdy mother and daughter shopping baskets include many of the techniques that you have already learned, as well as some new ones. Start with the smaller basket as it is easier to handle and keep in shape. When you have done this and are satisfied with the results you should feel confident enough to make the large version. Beads can be added or if you prefer you can leave the baskets plain. The larger basket will take longer to make. If the basket dries out and becomes difficult to handle you can always re-soak it until it becomes pliable.

The baskets

The smaller basket has a base diameter of 13cm (5in), height of sides, 11cm ($4\frac{1}{4}$in). The larger basket has a base diameter of 20cm (8in), height of sides, 19cm ($7\frac{1}{2}$in). The cane required for the baskets differs. As baskets get larger not only do they require more stakes but the cane must also be thicker to take the added weight. Cut six base sticks of No. 10 (3.35mm) cane, 13cm (5in) long. Point one end of three pieces and split the other three. Make a cross.

Pair with No.3 (2mm) cane for two rounds and then open the four arms to single sticks. Continue to pair until the work measures 11.5cm ($4\frac{1}{2}$in) across. Instead of making the base quite flat try to curve it to form a slight dome. This gives great strength to the basket and will prevent the bottom from falling out. Cut off any protruding base sticks and trim the surplus ends of the weavers. Cut 23 stakes for the sides of No. 8 (3mm) cane 41cm (16in) long. Slype (point) one end of each and insert a stake on each side of each base stick. Push the stakes into the weaving towards the centre. Note that there are 24 spaces and only 23 stakes are inserted. This is to get an odd number of stakes which makes randing easier. Leave the empty space where the base sticks are closest.

The upsett of a basket changes the direction at the base from going out to going up and it sets the shape for the rest of the basket whether it is straight up, flowing out, bowed or uneven.

Nip each stake close to the base with the round-nosed pliers (fig.1a) – make sure that the cane will bend easily and sharply without cracking. Nip the stakes in the correct direction to get them bending upwards. Bend all the stakes up with the dome shape of the base up on the inside. Tie the stakes at the top (fig.1b).

To continue with the small basket wale with three weavers (three rod wale). Push three weavers of No.5 (2.5mm) cane into the pairing of the base alongside three consecutive stakes. The stakes are now used singly. Don't make the mistake of keeping them in pairs.

Left: Wooden beads add colour to these shopping baskets.

Mark the stake immediately to the left of the first weaver so that you will know when to start the step-up on each round. Wale for four rounds but on the first round try to make the waling as close to the pairing as possible otherwise there will be gaps in the basket. After the first round the waling will build up on top of the previous round. Don't forget the step-up on each round and finish off correctly. Untie the stakes and place a weight inside the basket to control the shaping more easily.

Cut 23 bye-stakes of No.8 (3mm) cane 8cm (3in) long. Slype one end of each and insert one into the waling on the right side and in the same channel as each side stake. Rand with No.5 (2.5mm) cane for 5cm (2in) allowing the sides to lean out a little. Insert two 23cm (9in) handle liners, one on each side of the basket.

Wale for two rounds, with No.5 (2.5mm) cane and finish off if you are using beads. Cut off any surplus bye-stakes that protrude beyond the waling. If you are not using the beads wale for five rounds. Thread one bead onto each stake except the two where the handle liners are. Push them right down so that they are resting on the waling and are level. Wale on top of the beads for two rounds.

A rod border is a very neat and easily done border. It is sometimes called a commercial border because it is used more than any other by professional basket makers. Start with a three rod border – you can make thicker and bigger ones later. Re-soak the stakes and nip them with the round-nosed pliers 6mm ($\frac{1}{4}$in) above the waling to make them bend down easily without cracking. Nip them so that they bend sideways to the right.

Start the border anywhere you like. Bend a stake down to the right behind the next stake and back to the front. Repeat the same strokes with the next two stakes (fig.2). Go back to the first stake and pass it in front of the next upright stake and behind the next one and back to the front. Then bend the fourth stake down to the right to lie beside but behind the first stake (fig.3).

Repeat these movements with the second and fifth stakes and the third and sixth stakes. You should now have three pairs of stakes at the front – one long and one short cane to each pair (fig.4). Counting the bent down ends find the fifth one from the right –it will be the right hand one of the last pair – and take it in front of the next upright and behind the next and back to the front (the same movement as before) and bend the next upright (the seventh) down to lie beside and behind it. Repeat all the way round the basket – fifth from the right in front of one and behind one, and the next upright down beside it until there is only one upright left (fig.5). Work around the handle liners to make the border look as neat as possible. Aim to achieve a professional finish.

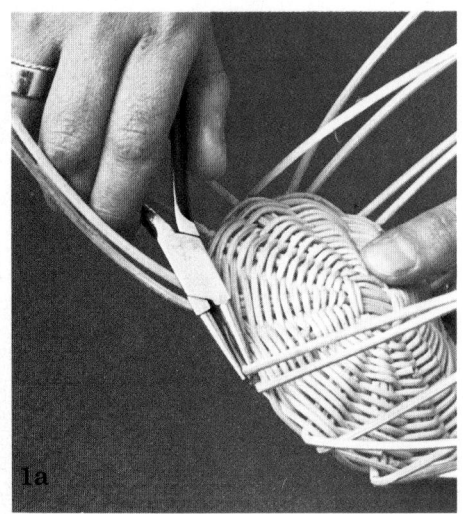

1a

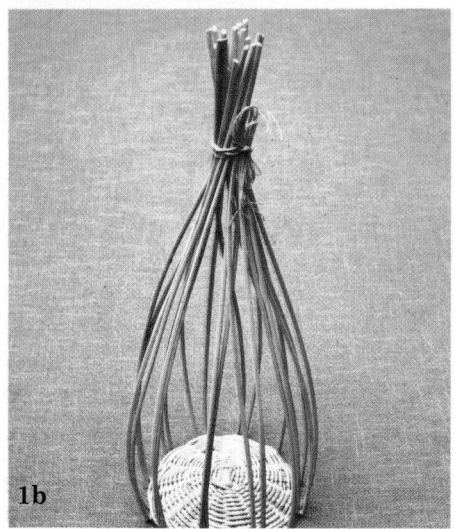

1b

Top: Nip cane with round-nosed pliers.
Above: Stakes gathered and tied at the top.

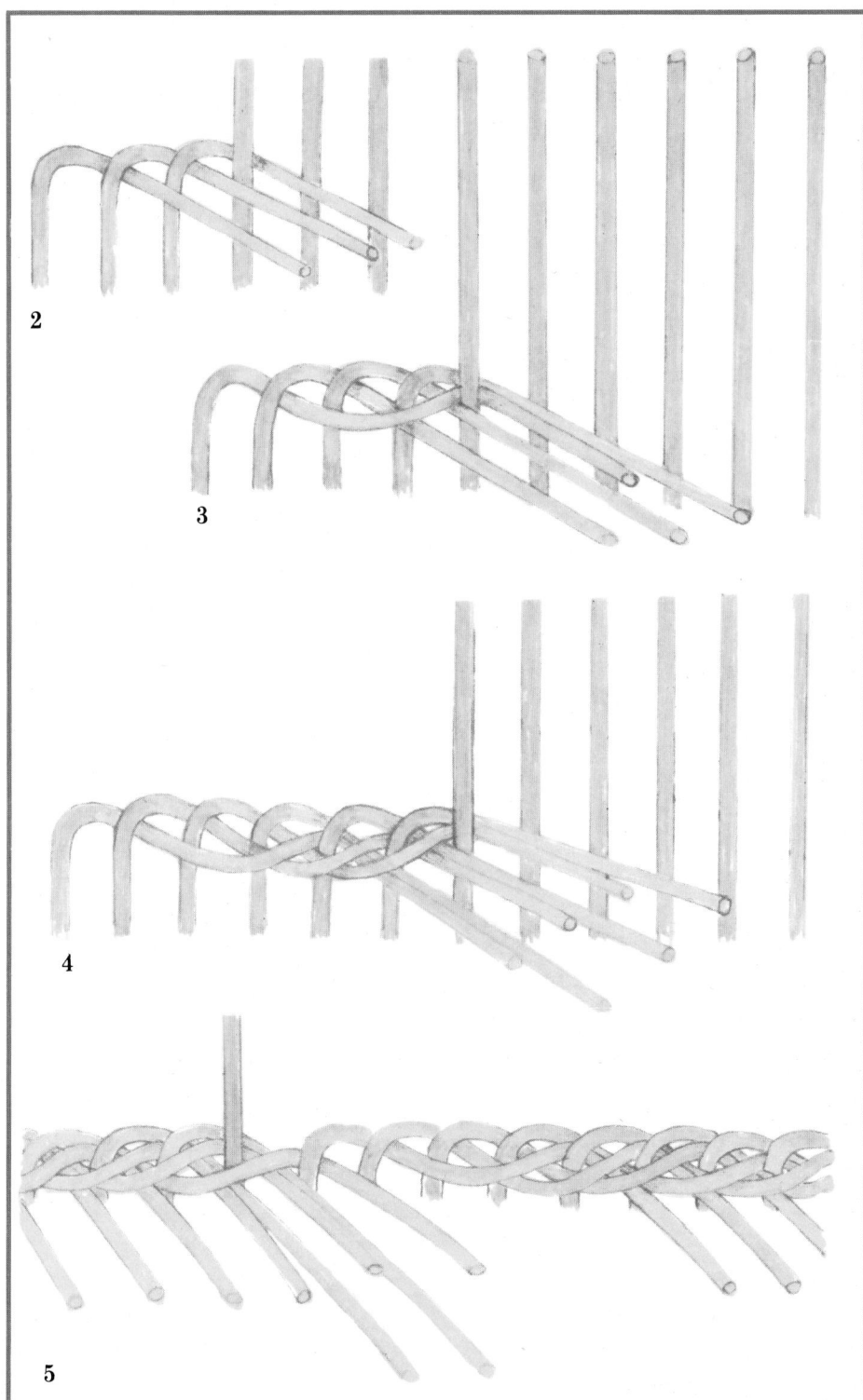

Small shopping basket

You will need:
28g (1oz) No.3 (2mm) cane.
56g (2oz) No.5 (2.5mm) cane.
113g (4oz) No.8 (3mm) cane.
1m (39in) No.10 (3.35mm) cane.
8mm (⅜in) handle cane 61cm (24in) long.
No.6 (2.6mm) chair seating cane, 5.5m (6yd) long.
61cm (24in) enamelled wrapping cane – optional.
21 wooden beads with holes to fit No.8 (3mm) cane.
Side-cutters.
Bodkin.
Round-nosed pliers.

2. First stage of three-rod border.
3. The first rod passes behind the fifth to form a pair with the fourth.
4. Three pairs of stakes are formed to the front of work.
5. The border is nearly complete, only one upright cane is left.

To finish the three rod border, again take the fifth from the right in front of one and under the elbow of the first cane and make the last upright bend down and under with it. You should still have three pairs to the front. The right hand stake of each of these pairs must be woven into the border in turn so that the border is complete and continuous. One stake comes to the front at each position all the way around. If you look at the top of the border where you began you will find that there are three single canes whereas all the rest of the rod border has two canes. Each of these single stakes has to have another cane lying with it and in front of it in order to complete the border. Check to see that this is so.

Take the fifth from the right and thread it under the elbow of the second stake that you bent down. Keep it in front of the first stake (fig.6). Now take the third from the right and thread it alongside (in front) of the next single cane and under the elbow of the third stake that you bent down. Lastly take the right hand one of the last pair and thread it alongside the last single cane and under the elbow of the fourth stake that you bent down.

There should now be one stake to the front evenly all the way round and these stakes should all be to the front at the bottom of the border. Make sure that the last three do not finish at the top of the border. You may finish your border here if you wish. Clip off all the surplus cane very close to the border. But if you want your basket to look very neat add a second simple border. This is called a follow-on trac border and is described below.

A follow-on trac border is made by threading each border stake in

6. Remaining canes are passed under canes which are already bent down.
7. A follow-on trac border leaves rod ends on the inside of the basket.

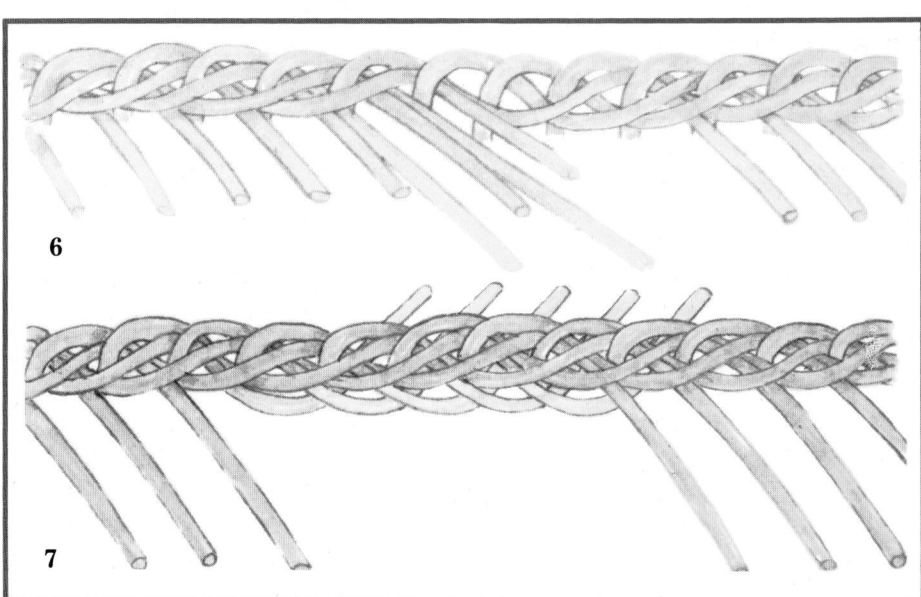

turn into the inside of the basket one or two spaces to the right and just above the waling under the other protruding stakes (fig.7).

Trim the ends of these stakes on the inside but be careful that the ends lie against a stake. If you cut them too short they will slip through back to the front of the basket.

For the handle Cut the handle cane to 53cm (21in) and soak it in hot water for 20 minutes. Slype both ends and shape the handle cane into a curve. Remove the handle liners and insert the bow into the holes made by the liners.

Wrap the handle with No.6 (2.6mm) chair seating cane using either the enamelled wrapping cane or a piece of chair seating cane to form a pattern across the handle. Finish the basket by pegging the handle as shown in the illustration.

The large basket

Proceed as for the smaller basket starting with eight base sticks No.12 (3.57mm) cane, 23cm (9in) long. Pair for two rounds with No.5 (2.5mm) cane and open the sticks into two's. Pair for another three rounds and open the sticks into singles. Continue pairing until the work measures 19cm (7½in) across.

Cut 31 stakes of No.10 (3.35mm) cane, 53cm (21in) long. Stake up and nip the stakes then wale for five rounds with No.6 (2.6mm) cane stepping up after each round.

Cut 31 bye-stakes of No.10 (3.35mm) cane, 15cm (6in) long and insert into the work as before. Rand for 10cm (4in) and insert handle liners. If you are not using the beads put on eight rounds of waling before making the border.

Put on four rounds of waling with No.6 (2.5mm) cane if you are using the beads. Then thread on the beads after trimming the protruding bye-stake ends. Add four more rounds of waling.

Make the trac border as before. Cut the handle cane 86.5cm (34in) long, soak and shape, slype both ends and insert into work. Wrap and peg as before to complete the basket.

Above left: The rod border as seen from above. The pattern is continued all the way around. Above right: A close-up detail showing the handle wrapping and securing peg.

Large shopping basket
You will need : 56g (2oz) No.5 (2.5mm) cane. 113g (4oz) No.6 (2.6mm) cane. 113g (4oz) No.10 (3.35mm) cane. No.12 (3.75mm) cane, 1.85m (2yd) long. No.10 (3.35mm) handle cane, 1m (39in) long. 5.5m (6yd) glossy wrapping cane or 8.3m (9yd) No.6 (2.6mm) chair seating cane. 1m (39in) enamelled cane – optional 29 wooden beads to thread onto No.10 (3.35mm) cane – optional. Side-cutters. Bodkin. Round-nosed pliers.

Oval tray and baskets

Baskets can be made round, oval and square and the designs are infinitely variable. Oval baskets are particularly versatile. A low oval basket, for example, is ideal for flowers or, instead of sloping sides, you can put a trac border on to the same base to make a table mat; then if made with higher sides it becomes a shopping basket.

But beware! Oval basketry is not easy, so practise with plenty of round baskets before you embark on this shape. Oval bases tend to twist, and reverse pairing has to be used as well as pairing to counteract the twist. For oval work some of the base sticks are longer than others and the longer ones are always threaded through the shorter ones. Although the longer sticks are often wrapped before the weaving is started, this is not essential.

This chapter introduces reverse pairing, four-rod waling and a rope handle which is very attractive.

To make an oval base
The base measures 19cm by 30.5cm (7½in by 12in) and can be used for the tray, the flower basket and the shopping basket.

Oval base
You will need : No.13 (4mm) cane, 3m (10ft) long. No.6 (2.6mm) chair seating cane, 1.22m (48in) long. No.5 (2.5mm) cane, 56g (2oz). Side-cutters. Bodkin. Round-nosed pliers.

Opposite: These baskets are made with an oval base. The bases are identical, but the sides are made differently.
Left: A view from the top of the oval basket, showing how the wrapping has been wound around the base sticks.

35

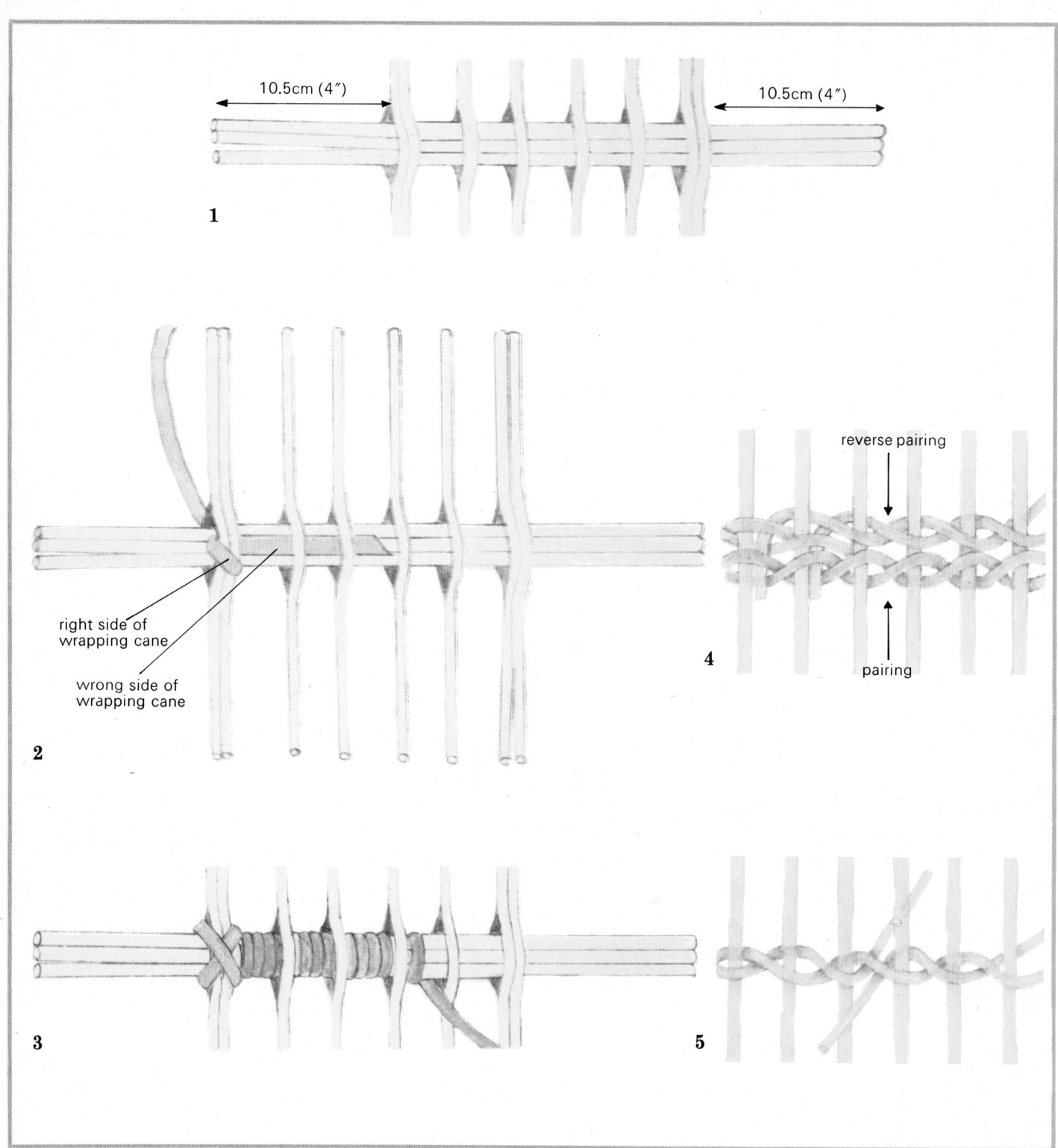

10.5cm (4″)

10.5cm (4″)

1

right side of
wrapping cane

wrong side of
wrapping cane

2

reverse pairing

pairing

4

3

5

Cut three sticks 32cm (13in) long and eight sticks 23cm (9in) long, all from No.13 (4mm) cane. Pierce the short sticks in the centre and thread the three longer ones through. Arrange the sticks (fig.1).

Wrapping – this is optional and need not be done for your first few baskets. Wrap the long sticks with No.6 (2.6mm) chair seating cane. Thread a piece of chair seating cane, wrong side uppermost, into the splits of the short ends. This will become the underside of the basket (fig.2). Wrap the cane around the double outer sticks so that it forms a cross on the upper side of the base.

Wrap the long sticks between the short sticks. See that there are the same number of wraps between each of the short sticks (fig.3). Finish with a matching cross at the other end and thread the end of the chair seating cane under the wrapping for a few centimetres (inches). Now your sticks are ready.

Pair with No.5 (2.5mm) cane. Loop the cane around the long sticks at one end of the base (as for a round base). Pair around the base for two rounds and keep the work straight and not sloping to one side. Weave close to the base sticks all around. Open all the sticks to form single spokes and then continue to pair for a further 4.5cm (1¾in). Make the right side of the base concave and try not to let the work twist. Keep all the short sticks, except the two outer ones, straight while you are pairing.

Reverse pairing Insert two pieces of No.5 (2.5mm) cane into base to right of two consecutive base sticks where the pairing ended. Hold the two canes at back of the work. Take the left hand weaver behind one stick and in front of the next – over the top of the other weaver – then to the back again. In other words, it is exactly the opposite of pairing. Each stroke must finish with both canes at the back (fig.4).

Join in a new cane in the same way as for pairing but push the new cane into position from the back so that the new end is at the front and the old one at the back (fig.5).

Reverse pair for 4.5cm (1¾in). *The amount of reverse pairing must always equal the amount of pairing so that the twist is completely counteracted.* The base should now measure 19cm by 30cm (7½in by 12in). Trim all the ends of the weavers close to the work and also trim the protruding ends of the sticks. This completes the base and you can add a trac border to make a table mat or continue and make a tray, flower basket or shopping basket.

The tray

The tray is the same size as the base, 19cm by 30cm (7½in by 12in) with sides 6cm (2¼in) high plus the two handles.
Make the base as before. Cut 31 stakes of No.10 (3.35mm) cane,

1. *The long sticks are threaded through the shorter ones.*
2. *The chair seating cane is threaded as shown to start the wrapping.*
3. *The cane is wrapped around each short section equally.*
4. *Reverse pairing is used to counteract the twist when pairing is used for oval work.*
The top row shows the cane inserted in the pairing.
5. *Joining the cane in reverse pairing.*

Tray
You will need : (The materials include the cane needed for the base.) No.13 (4mm) cane, 3m (10ft) long. No.10 (3.35mm) cane, 85g (3oz). No.6 (2.6mm) chair seating cane, 28g (1oz). No.6 (2.6mm) cane, 56g (2oz). No.5 (2.5mm) cane, 56g (2oz). 8mm (5⁄16in) handle cane, 61cm (24in) long. Handle liners. Side-cutters. Bodkin. Round-nosed pliers.

Flower basket

You will need:
(The materials include the cane needed for the base.)
No.13 (4mm) cane, 3m (10ft) long.
No.10 (3.35mm) cane, 113g (4oz).
No.6 (2.6mm) chair seating cane, 1.22m (48in) long.
No.6 (2.6mm) cane, 113g (4oz).
No.5 (2.5mm) cane, 113g (4oz).
8mm ($\frac{5}{16}$in) handle cane, 66cm (26in) long.
Handle liners.
Side-cutters.
Bodkin.
Round-nosed pliers.

38cm (15in) long. Point one end of each and insert them into the base in the following order: one on each side of each of the long sticks at both ends and one on each side of each of the outside short sticks at both ends, and one beside each of the remaining short sticks. You will find that you are one stake short. As for the round bases, one stick is missing where the sticks are closest, to give you an odd number to work with.

Nip the stakes close to the base and bend them up with the dome shape of the base uppermost. Tie the stakes together to keep them in order while you upsett. Use four weavers of No.6 (2.6mm) cane for this upsett as it needs to be sturdier than for round baskets. Insert the weavers into the base weaving beside four consecutive stakes, along one side of the base. You are now ready to wale.

Four-rod wale by taking the left hand weaver in front of three stakes and behind one stake and back to the front. Use each left hand weaver in turn. Try to part the stakes at each end so that they are all evenly spaced and make the weavers go under the basket, close to the pairing, before going behind the next stake.

Mark the stake to the left of the very first weaver as you did for a three-rod wale. Wale all the way around until a weaver passes around the marked stake. Cut this weaver off leaving about 15cm (6in) so that it can be woven to the inside of the basket later. Step-up with remaining three weavers. Continue with a three-rod wale – in front of two and behind one – until the sides measure 5cm (2in). Now thread the fourth weaver that you cut off at the end of the first round, into the inside of the basket. It will fill a small gap.

Put a weight inside the basket to steady it. You will find it easier to manipulate and shape the work. Insert two handle liners at each end of the tray with 9cm ($3\frac{1}{2}$in) between each pair.

A four-rod border is exactly the same as a three-rod border except that you bend down four stakes to the right, each behind the next stake and back to the front again. As you weave you will always have four pairs to the front instead of three (for a three-rod border) and at the end there will be four weavers to weave into the beginning of the border instead of three. If you are very ambitious and skilful you can try a five-rod border – bend down five to start, always have five pairs and weave five at the end. The greater the number of rods, the thicker and sturdier the border becomes. Use No.10 (3.35mm) cane. Put on a follow-on trac border if you wish as it does give a neat finish to your work.

Cut two pieces of handle cane 30cm (12in) long, soak well and curve them into bow shapes. Slype both ends of the bow so that the cuts come on the inside of the bow. Remove handle liners and insert the handle. Wrap the handle and peg it to finish.

Flower basket

Using the same base as before, the sides of this basket are 10cm (4in) high plus the rope handle.

Make an oval base exactly as before. Cut 31 stakes 48cm (19 in) long of No.10 (3.35mm) cane. Although this basket is only 5cm (2in) higher than the tray, it flows out more which means that the border stakes will be wider apart and the border will therefore need more cane. You are now ready to insert the stakes.

Insert the stakes into the base as for the tray. Nip the stake ends and upsett with a four-rod wale for one round and continue with a three-rod wale for four more rounds in the usual manner.

Cut 31 bye-stakes of No.10 (3.35mm) cane 13cm (5in) long, point one end of each and insert them into the waling – one to the right of each stake. Using No.6 (2.6mm) cane, rand for 8cm (3in) trying to bend the ends of the basket well out but keeping the sides straight up. Don't forget that a stone or weight in your basket will help to keep it steady and make it easier to shape the work.

Put in handle liners, one on each side of the basket. Wale for four rounds still shaping the ends outwards. Put on a three, four, or five-

Above left: The canes are inserted next to the handle cane to start the rope effect.
Above right: Wrapping the handle. Canes are passed around the handle cane to the opposite side.
Below left: Once the handle cane is covered, each cane is used separately and threaded around the handle to create the herring-bone pattern to finish the basket.

rod border and a follow-on trac border if you like. Cut one piece of handle cane 66cm (36in) long, shape into a bow and slype each end. Remove the handle liners and insert the handle.

For the rope handle Cut 10 pieces of No.5 (2.5mm) cane 96.5cm (38in) long, point one end of each and insert five beside the handle bow at each end. Insert them into the top of the border and to the left of the bow at each end. Make them follow the bow around.

Start at one side and take that set of handle weavers across in front of the bow – to the right – then wrap them round the bow three or four times, over to the other side. Leave the ends of these canes inside the basket. Repeat with the other set of weavers on the other side, taking these weavers into the spaces between the first set. Take care to keep them all in the correct order and do not let them twist at all. When both sets of weavers are in place there may be gaps or 'grins' in between the canes. If so cut two more weavers and insert one on each side – to the right of the original set – and following the roping effect as before. Repeat with two more if necessary. If the handle gets filled up in places but not in others, it means that the initial roping was not even. Start again and have another go. Push all the weaver ends through the waling, from the inside to the outside of the basket and to the right of the handle bow underneath the waling. Again be sure to keep these weavers in the correct order.

To make the herringbone finish these weavers have to be taken up and around the back of the handle and back to the front again. Use one weaver at a time. Hold the basket with one side towards you so that the ends of the weavers will be protruding on the right of the handle bow. Take the first (or left hand) weaver, up and across the waling, over the border on the left of the handle, around the back of the handle and back down and across the waling. Push this weaver to the inside of the basket on the left of the handle, again underneath the waling. Use each weaver in turn. Make sure that the crosses all come even, each one higher than the last.

Weaving away – when all the weavers are inside the basket weave them in and out of the waling to finish them off. This is called weaving away. Repeat the herringbone pattern on the other side and weave away using exactly the same method.

Shopping basket

A shopping basket is made by a combination of the two previous baskets. Make the base exactly as before. Cut stakes 45cm (18in).

Upsett, wale, bye-stake, rand and top-wale as for the flower basket, but keep the sides quite straight. Put one handle liner at each end. Put one the same border as before and add the rope handle from end to end to finish the basket.

Above: Details of the rope handle showing the inside view and the herring-bone pattern on the outside.
Opposite: A doll's cradle with a plait [braid] border involves new techniques and careful weaving.

Packing and chain pairing

A very pleasant way of learning new basketry techniques is to make the doll's cradle illustrated. The base for the cradle can be made exactly like the oval base described in the last chapter or you can alter it and learn a new technique.

The new techniques in this chapter are chain pairing, plait [braid] borders and packing. The chain pairing on the base is not essential but it is attractive and not at all difficult. The plaited [braided] border looks difficult but follow the instructions carefully and you will get it right the first time. Packing means building up one side of a basket so that it is higher than the rest and creates different levels.

The cradle

The cradle is 30cm (11¾in) high and 37cm (14½in) long. The rockers are not essential so if you can't work with wood don't let it deter you from making the cradle.

Cut three sticks 32cm (13in) long and eight sticks 23cm (9in) long, from No.13 (4mm) cane, to make the base. Pierce and thread the sticks and wrap with chair seating cane as shown previously.

Chain pairing To prevent oval work from twisting, an equal number of pairing and reverse pairing rounds are put on the base. If these techniques are used on alternate rows they form a chain pattern which is extremely attractive.

Working from a long end pair with No.5 (2.5mm) cane for half a round only. Loop a second weaver round next stick beyond the pairing and reverse pair until you reach the pairing weavers. Drop the reverse pairing weavers and continue pairing with the pairing weavers until you reach the reverse pairing weavers again. Continue in this way, alternating the pairs of weavers, and never letting either pair overtake the other. Keep the reverse pairing weavers at the back of the work and the pairing weavers to the front. You are now ready to open the sticks.

Open all the sticks to singles on the third round and make the base slightly concave. Continue chain pairing until the work measures 19cm by 30cm (7½in by 12in). Trim surplus weavers and sticks.

For the upsetting you will need 31 stakes of No.10 (3.35mm) cane. These will differ in length. Half the number, say 15, must be shorter and will go around the foot of the cradle – cut these 52cm (20in) long. The longer ones, the remaining 16, go around the hood and must gradually increase in length. Cut two lengths of each starting at 53cm (21in) and then in increments of 2.5cm (1in). The length of these stakes varies according to how high and how far over you want the hood to be. See illustration on page 41.

Point one end of each stake and insert the pointed ends into the base. Make sure that the slight dome on the base will be inside the

Doll's cradle

You will need :
56g (2oz) No.13 (4mm) cane.
170g (6oz) No.10 (3.35mm) cane.
56g (2oz) No.5 (2.5mm) cane.
170g (6oz) No.6 (2.6mm) cane.
No.6 (2.6mm) chair seating cane, 1.85m (2yd), long.
Side-cutters.
Bodkin.
Round-nosed pliers.

For the rockers :
2 pieces of softwood 50mm by 25mm (2in by 1in), 28cm (11in) long – optional.
4 No. 10 brass screws 25mm (1in) long with washers or screw cups to attach rockers to basket.
Surform tool to shape rockers.
Saw and fine grade sandpaper.

basket. Be careful to keep the longer ones together at one end and in the correct order and position for the hood. Nip each stake close to the base pairing, so that they bend up easily without cracking. Tie the stakes together in two bunches – one bunch at the foot and the other at the head. This is to make the upsetting easier and to avoid distorting the base of the cradle.

Insert four weavers of No.6 (2.6mm) cane into the base and do a four-rod wale for one round. Change to a three-rod wale for five rounds remembering to step-up on each round.

Cut 31 bye-stakes of No.10 (3.35mm) cane, half of them 13cm (5in) long and half gradually increasing, as for the stakes, to a maximum of 28cm (11in). Point one end of each and insert the pointed ends into the waling of the upsetting, one beside, and to the right, of each stake. Keep the longest bye-stake beside the longest stake etc, in order, all the way around.

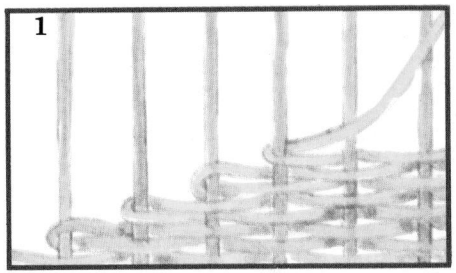

Above: To make the hood one side of the basket is packed. A weaver is taken around a decreasing number of stakes.

Rand with No.6 (2.6mm) cane for 5cm (2in). Allow the sides to flow out a little and the ends slightly more. Using No.6 (2.6mm) cane put on two rounds of three-rod waling.

Packing – this is done to make the hood. Start randing with No.6 (2.6mm) cane, at the head of the cradle and weave to the right until you reach the middle of the side. Turn the weaver right around the next stake and weave back towards the head, all the way around, until you reach the middle of the other side. Turn the weaver right around the next stake so that it is facing the head end again.

Continue randing to the other side to one stake less than on the previous round. Turn the weaver around again and weave to the other side, again to one stake less than on previous round (fig.1). Repeat this weaving backwards and forwards going around one stake less each time on both sides so that the head end grows higher. Push the stakes forwards as you weave to form the hood. Continue until you are turning the weaver around the two longest stakes. Leave the weaver on the inside of the work.

Using No.6 (2.6mm) cane wale for two rounds all the way around the cradle and then repeat the packing procedure exactly as before. (For a bigger hood you can repeat the packing process a third time if you wish.) Finally put on two more rounds of waling using No.6 (2.6mm) cane. Trim any surplus bye-stakes and weavers – *not the stakes*. You can now complete the cradle with a three-rod border if you wish but a plait [braid] border is more decorative.

Plait [braid] border Keep the work well soaked and if you make a mistake don't be discouraged, undo the work and try again, the result is well worth the effort and time involved.

Using No.10 (3.35mm) cane cut three pieces 25cm (10in) long and two pieces 8cm (3in) long. The long canes are substitute stakes and will be replaced by the real ones at the end. The short canes are merely cushions so that the first canes are not bent down too low and will allow space to thread the last stakes under these 'elbows' at the end of the border. They are removed later.

Nip all the stakes 6mm ($\frac{1}{4}$in) above the waling so that they bend over easily to the right. Starting at the foot end (the easiest place) place one of the 8cm (3in) canes against a stake at right angles to the waling and bend the first stake down to the front over it. Place a 25cm (10in) substitute cane alongside the stake. Leave 5cm (2in) sticking into the inside. Repeat with the other 8cm (3in) cane against

2. Short pieces of cane leave room for threading finishing ends which also replace the substitute canes.
3. Left hand pair goes over next pair into the inside leaving an upright stake to its left which is bent down and coupled with a substitute cane.

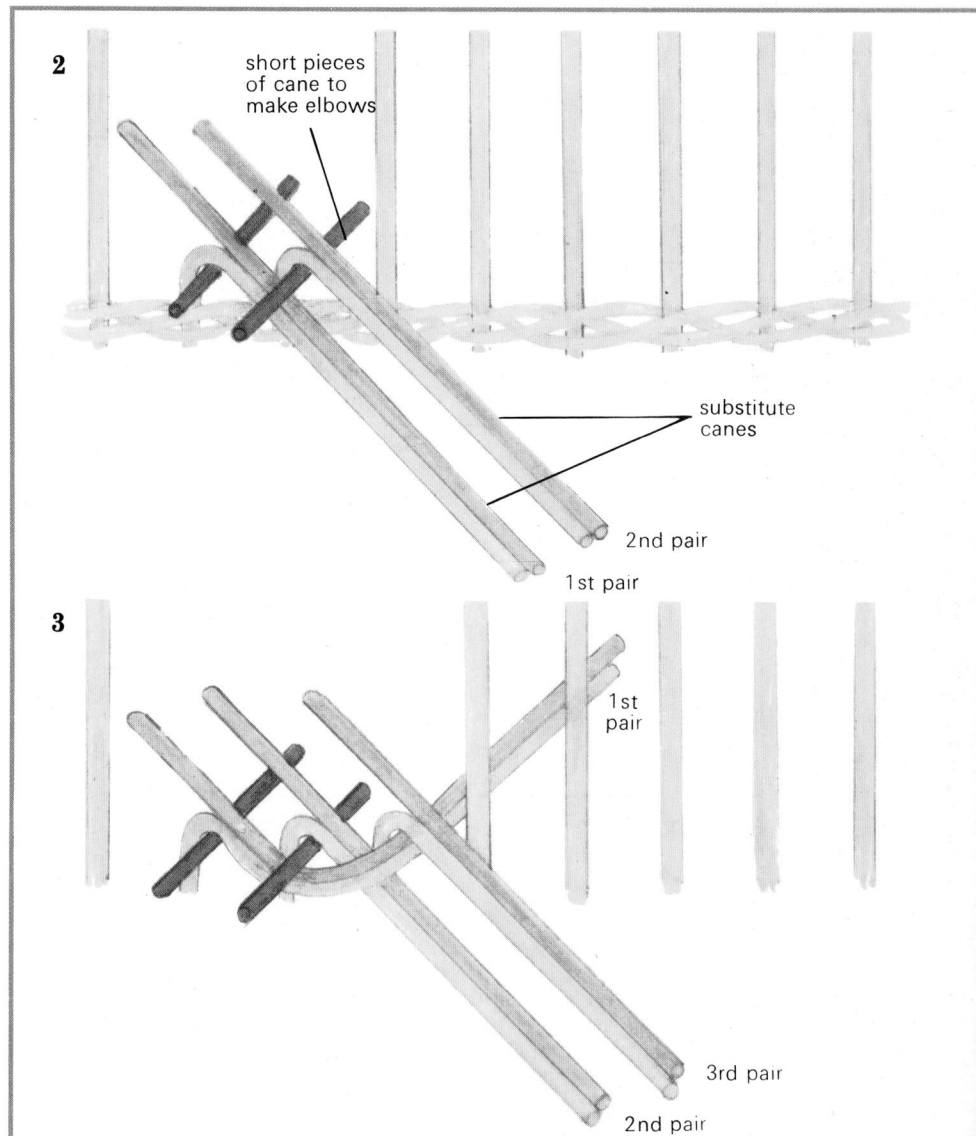

2 short pieces of cane to make elbows

substitute canes

2nd pair

1st pair

3 1st pair

3rd pair

2nd pair

44

the next stake to the right and bend that stake down over it and place the second substitute cane behind it (fig.2).

Take the first left hand pair over the second pair and in between the next two upright stakes, into the centre of the basket. Bend the third stake down to the front over this pair and place the third substitute cane beside and alongside this stake (fig.3). Take the second pair over the third pair and between the next two upright stakes into the centre. Bend the fourth stake down to the front (fig.4). Bring the left hand pair on the inside of the work back to the front to lie beside, but behind, the stake you have just bent down

4. *The second pair goes over next pair and in between the next two upright stakes to the right.*
5. *The first pair goes over the second pair on its way to the front to lie next to the fourth stake.*

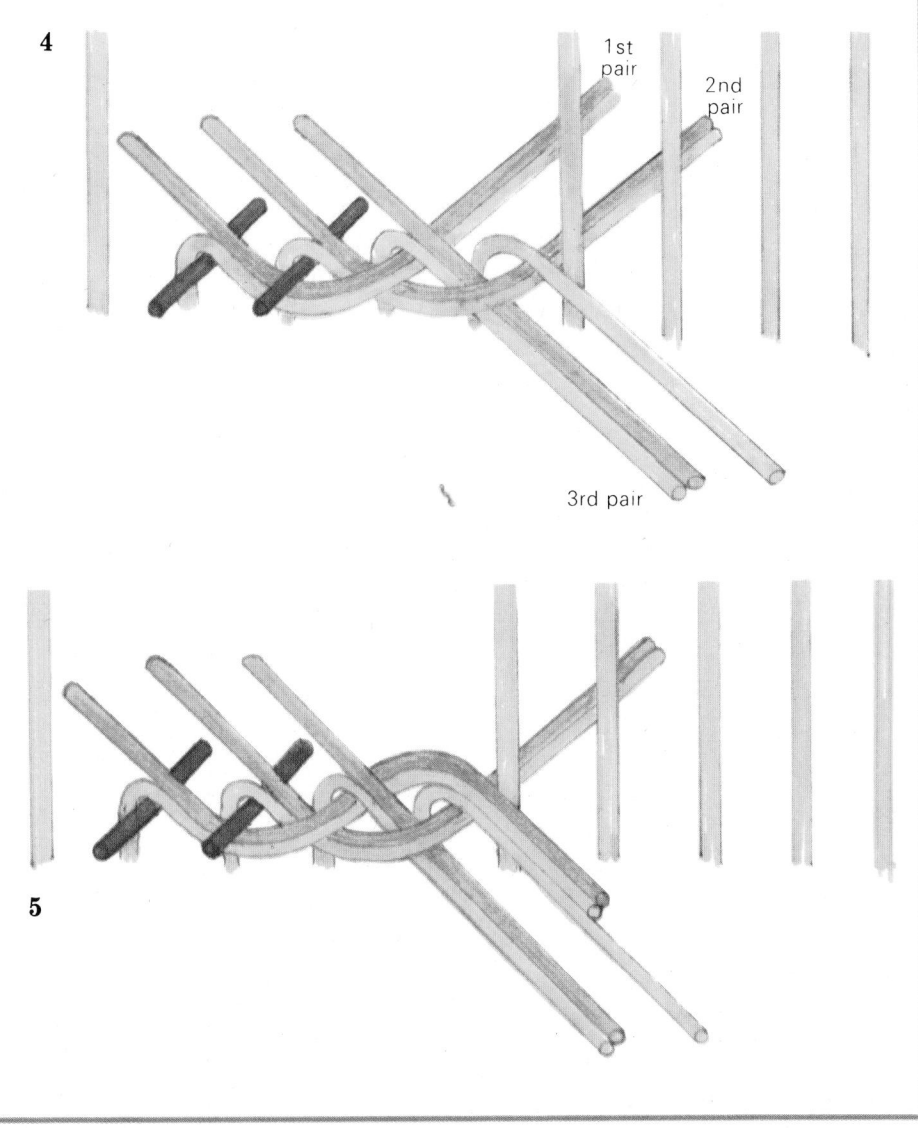

4

1st
pair

2nd
pair

3rd pair

5

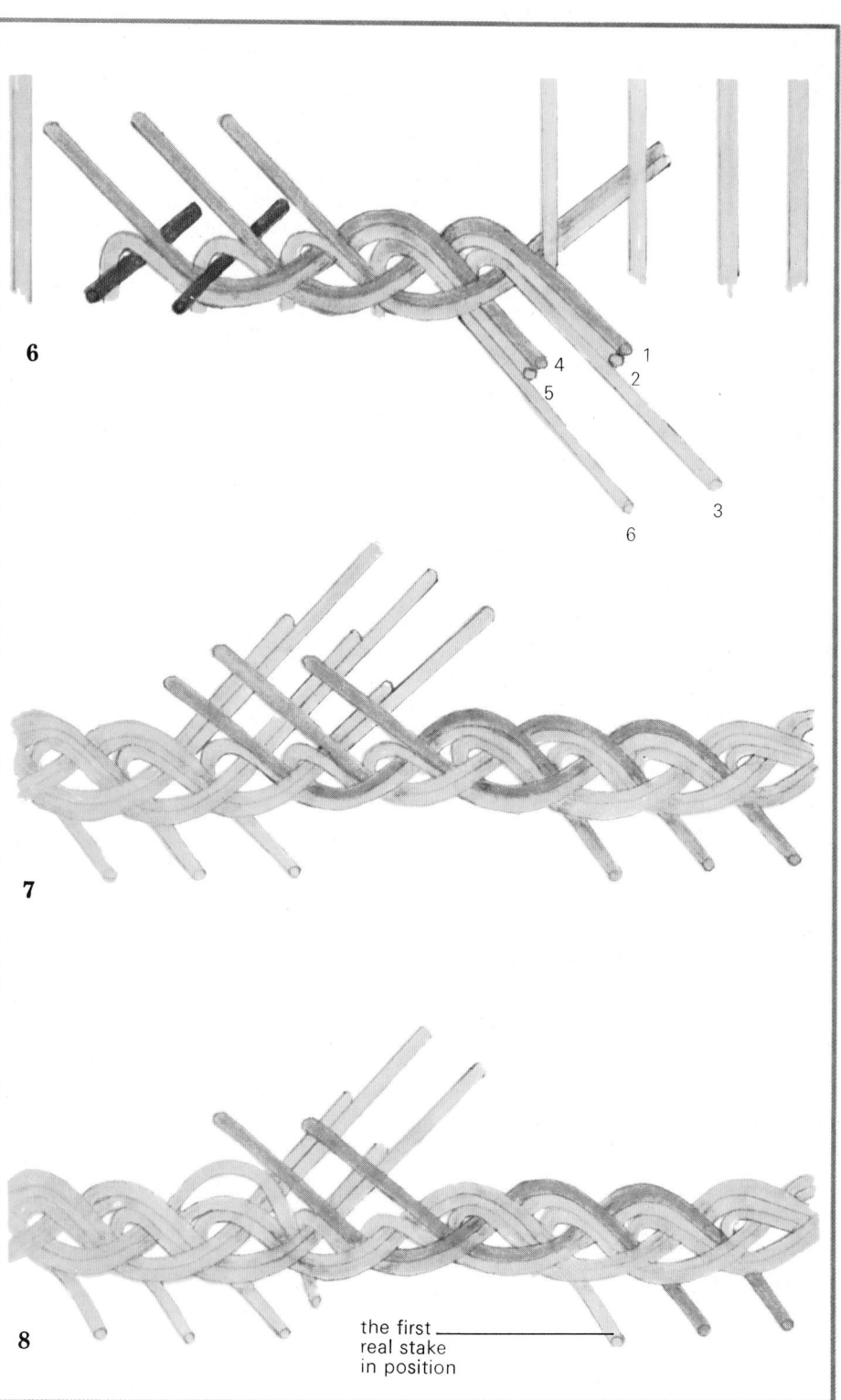

6. *The third pair goes to the inside and the second pair comes out over it to lie next to the fifth stake.*

7. *The short bits of cane are removed and now the real stakes must take the place of the substitute canes.*

8. *The first substitute cane is removed in stages and the longer stake of the pair is threaded in position.*

the first real stake in position

(fig.5). Repeat the last stroke with the third pair and once again the inside left hand pair is brought out to lie beside and behind the fifth stake as illustrated in fig.6.

From now on you will have two pairs on the inside. Always bring the left hand one out, after you have turned down the next stake. At the same time you will have two sets of three canes to the front. Counting these canes from the right, take the fifth and sixth cane each time, to the inside of the basket, in between the next two upright stakes, and over the top of the first four canes.

Say to yourself, 'five and six go in, next stake down and left hand pair comes out'. If it goes wrong and you suddenly have a cane that is too short to complete its stroke, it is because you have twisted the canes around as you passed them in or out of the basket. Repeat all the away around making sure that you turn each stake down close to the waling. Don't leave gaps between the border and the waling. Continue until you have bent the last stake down and the left hand inside pair comes out.

To finish the border remove the first 8cm (3in) cane (if it has not already fallen out) and thread the fifth and sixth cane from the right under the elbow of the second stake (fig.7). There are now three pairs on the inside – a long cane and a short cane to each pair. Each of the right hand canes (the long ones) is the real stake that is to replace each of the substitute ones. Keep them in the right order.

Remove the left hand or first substitute cane bit by bit and weave the real cane into its place. Don't remove so much of the substitute cane at any one time that you lose the place where the real one goes (fig.8). Repeat this with the centre and remaining right hand canes. Now you have three odd canes on the inside of the basket. Thread each of these one 'plait' [braid] to the right and through the border to the front. The finished border will now look continuous all the way round. Trim off the ends of the canes as close to the plait [braid] as possible. This makes them unobtrusive.

To make the rockers saw the two pieces of wood with a diagonal cut at each end as shown (fig.9). Round the corners off with a Surform. Smooth the curve with fine sand-paper.

Decide on exactly the right position for the rockers and the screws to be attached to the cradle. For the screws gouge holes 8.5cm (3⅜in) from each end of each rocker, on the upper flat surface, with a bodkin or a bradawl. Varnish the rockers. Push the screws through the screw cups or washers so that they match the holes in the rockers. Be careful not to split any of the base sticks or weavers with the screws. Tighten the screws to secure the rockers in position. As pointed out before, it is not strictly necessary to make rockers if you are not confident in your skills at woodwork.

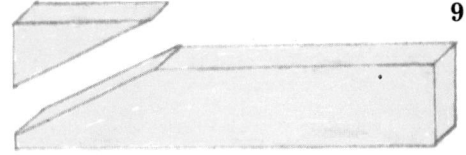

9

Above: Diagonal saw cuts remove waste. Corners are filed around.

Below: Detail of the screws in position.
Bottom: Rockers are attached to bottom of the cradle.

Making oval
wine cradles

The wine cradles illustrated are made with oval bases. The techniques involve packing one end to support the top of the bottle and a variation of it making a recess for the neck of the bottle. Two types of handles are made. The first type consists of two flexible curved handles and the other is a secure T-shaped handle. The completed cradles can be dyed or stained with wood stains if you wish. You can also design your own baskets.

For example you can pack both ends of the oval base to make a fruit or flower basket. Make a cross handle and wrap it with chair seating cane or use cane for a rope effect.

Cradle with curved handles

The base of the cradle measures 17cm by 10.5cm (6¾in by 4¼in) and after packing, it is 27cm (10½in) long.

For the base cut six sticks 11.5cm (4½in) long and three sticks 18cm (7in) long, all from No.10 (3.35mm) cane. Pierce the short sticks in the centre and thread the long ones through to form an oval pattern with the short sticks grouped in the centre with a space of 1.6cm (⅝in) between each. Wrap the long sticks with No.2 (1.85mm) chair seating cane – this is optional.

Pair and reverse pair with No.3 (2mm) cane so that the base measures 15cm by 9.5cm (6in by 3¾in). Make the base slightly concave – the dome will form the inside of the basket. Put on the pairing and the reverse pairing in any pattern, but use an equal number of rounds of each. Chain pair if you wish – it is very attractive. Trim surplus base sticks once base weaving is completed.

Begin upsetting by cutting 27 stakes of No.8 (3mm) cane, 16 of these must be 30cm (12in). Gradually increase the length of the remaining 11 to a maximum of 35cm (14in). This is for the forward end, or front, which juts out and is slightly higher than the rest of the basket to hold the bottle.

Point one end of each stake and insert them into the base so that the odd one out is a short stake at the back of the basket. The longer stakes are arranged around the front end with the longest stake in the centre. Nip the stakes close to the base weaving and bend them upwards. Tie them together at the top. Upsett with one round of four-rod waling continue with a three-rod wale for two rounds, all with No.6 (2.6mm) cane. Step-up after each round.

Cut 27 bye-stakes of No.5 (2.5mm) cane, 21 of these are 10cm (4in) long and the remaining six are 30cm (12in) long. Point one end of each and insert them into the upsetting, one on the right side of

Left: These wine cradles are made in the same way, except for the different styles of handles.

49

Below: Detail showing the packing to form the lip.

each stake. The longer bye-stakes must be arranged at the front with the longer stakes. These long bye-stakes will eventually become 'stakes' to help form the lip of the basket.

Put on ten rounds of randing with No.6 (2.6mm) cane. Keep the sides and the back going up vertically but ease the front stakes slightly forwards and outwards. Wale for three rounds with No.6 (2.6mm) cane when shaping the front of the basket. Put on six rounds of randing with No.5 (2.5mm) cane and keep shaping the front. Finer cane is used for this randing so that it is easier to shape the lip or front of the basket. On the next round of randing, divide the six long stakes and bye-stakes at the front, so that they become singles. Rand for two more rounds keeping the front stakes single and shaping the lip well to the front.

Packing Build up the lip by randing backwards and forwards with No.5 (2.5mm) cane. Start at the fifth stake from the centre of the back and weave towards the front, around the front of the fifth stake before the centre of the back. Bend the weaver right around this stake and weave back along the previous round but to one stake less than from where you started. Keep repeating this, randing backwards and forwards, one stake less each time on both sides, until you are only weaving around the last two stakes. Keep shaping the lip while doing this. Leave the end of the weaver inside the basket. Wale all the way around with No.6 (2.6mm) cane for two rounds. Trim all the surplus ends of the *21 shorter bye-stakes*. Be careful not to cut off the six longer bye-stakes, they are for the border.

Border Re-soak the stakes if necessary and nip them 6mm ($\frac{1}{4}$in) above the waling. Put on a four-rod border. Trim all the surplus stakes and weavers with the side cutters.

Handles Cut two pieces of 8mm ($\frac{5}{16}$in) handle cane 53cm (21in) long. Make a tongue at both ends of each by cutting away most of the thickness of the cane on one side (fig.1). Start the cuts 15cm (6in) in from the ends. Don't make the usual slanting cut but cut away quite sharply and then straight down to form a tongue. Both cuts on each handle piece must face the same way.

Soak the cane well and bend it to the shape you require. Push the two tongues into the basket from the outside and underneath the top waling. Position them as illustrated, near the fourth stake from the back and the front. Bend the tongues up and over the border to meet the main part of the handle (fig.2). Keep the 'eyelet' that is formed round by shaping it with your fingers or by bending it around the handle of a bodkin. Make sure both handles are the same length and height as one another.

Secure the tongues to main part of the handles with adhesive tape and leave work to dry. Remove adhesive tape and stick into

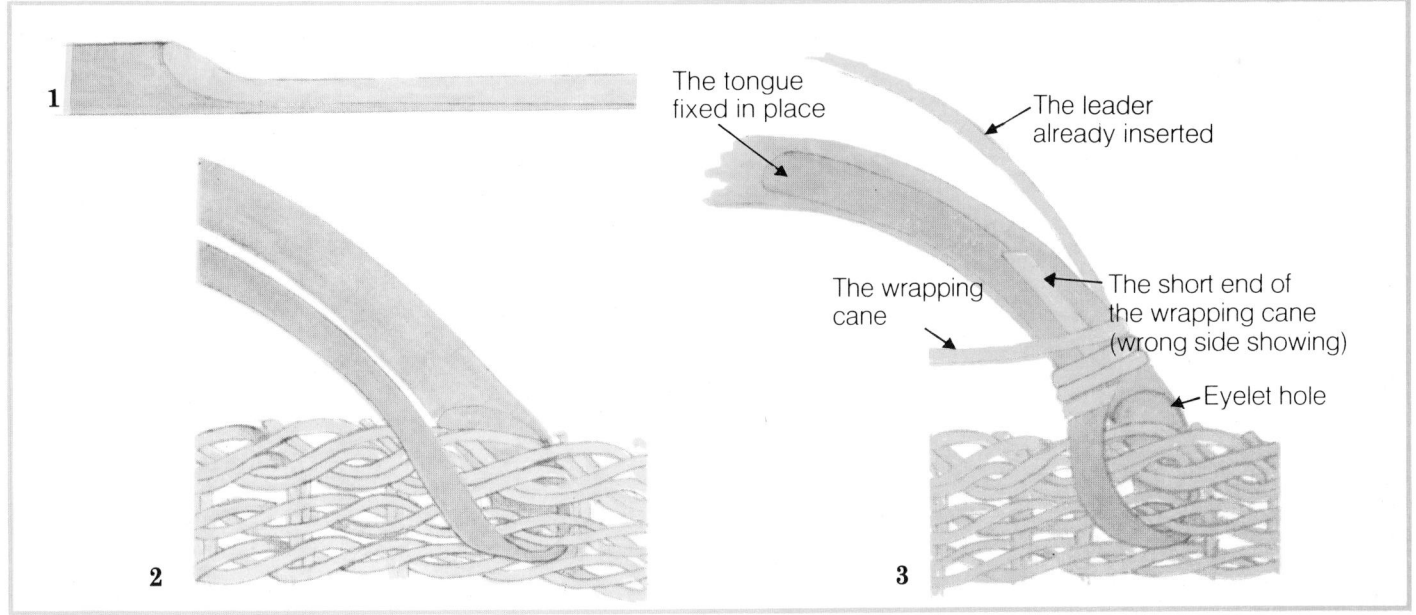

1
2
3

The tongue
fixed in place

The leader
already inserted

The wrapping
cane

The short end of
the wrapping cane
(wrong side showing)

Eyelet hole

position with all-purpose adhesive, secure again with adhesive tape until dry. Wrap each handle with No.6 (2.6mm) chair seating cane. Bend this cane about 5cm (2in) from one end so that it forms an L-shape just above the eyelet, ie where the tongue joins the handle (fig.3). This gives you a firm start.

You are now ready to start wrapping with the long end. Put a piece of chair seating cane in the work to go over the top of the handle and wrap it in with the short end around the handle. Continue wrapping, making any pattern you wish with the leader. Wrap across to the other side to the edge of the eyelet hole to finish with four plain rounds of wrapping.

Finish by tucking the end back up inside the wrapping. This is done by loosening the wrapping and pulling the end through and then tightening the wrapping again. It can also be secured by pushing it through the join by the tongue and the handle and keeping it in position with all-purpose adhesive once the cane is dry. Repeat for the other handle and finish with four plain rounds of wrapping.

1. The handle cane is cut as shown to form a tongue shape.
2. The tongue is pushed through the weaving and folded back.
3. The tongue is secured by wrapping with chair seating cane.

Cradle with T-handle

The base for this cradle is made exactly like the one for the previous cradle. The size is similar but this one has a plait [braid] border with a recess for the neck of the bottle in the packing. You can change the design and put on the handles used in the previous cradle if you wish. The borders are also interchangeable.

Make the base as before. Upsett and continue as for the previous cradle until you have to cut the bye-stakes.

Cut 27 bye-stakes of No.8 (3mm) cane – 16 must be 10cm (4in) long and the remaining eleven must gradually increase to a maximum length of 18cm (7in). Point one end of each and insert them into the waling, one on the right side of each stake. Arrange them so that the longer ones are at the front and in the correct order. Rand for ten rounds with No.6 (2.6mm) cane. Insert the handle liners, one in the centre back and the other two – one on either side – at the sixth cane from the front. These two must be more than halfway towards the front to balance the basket when tipped to pour.

Cut two pieces of 8mm ($\frac{5}{16}$ in) cane 15cm (6in) long. Point one end of each and soak them well. Insert these two sticks into the weaving at the front to form the edges of the opening. Insert them next to the two stakes that are immediately to the left and right of the centre stake so that only one stake is left in the middle. Remove and discard the bye-stakes if necessary to insert the sticks more readily. Bend the sticks well forward into the shape that you intend for the opening. Rand with No.6 (2.6mm) cane all the way around for nine rounds. Press the front stakes forwards.

Packing Build up the front as before, but this time leave a gap in the work. Start as before at the fifth stake from the back and rand as far as the thick stick at the front. Wind the cane around that stick and back along the same side to one stake less. Every other time you pass the thick stick pass the cane around it twice so that it builds up well and completely covers the stick (fig.4).

Continue like this until you are weaving around the last two stakes. Leave the cane on the inside of the work. Repeat on the other side and make sure both sides are the same height. Put four more rounds of randing on each side by working backwards and forwards. The gap at the front should now be about 4.5cm (1$\frac{3}{4}$in) deep to leave space for the bottle neck.

Insert three weavers of No.6 (2.6mm) cane next to the first three stakes next to the gap at the front. Wale right around to the other side, cut off the weavers and insert the ends into the weaving. Cut off all the surplus bye-stakes including the one at the front in between the two thick sticks. Re-soak the two thick sticks if necessary and cut them off so that they are level with the weaving.

Border Cut four pieces of No.8 (3mm) cane, 20cm (8in) long and point one end of each. These are border stakes for the gap. Insert two into each thick stick one 12mm ($\frac{1}{2}$in) from the top and one 13mm ($\frac{1}{2}$in) from the bottom of the gap. Insert them by making a hole in the stick with the bodkin and pushing the pointed end of the border stake into the hole (fig.5). Make sure that they are firmly in place. If not, make the holes bigger and try again.

Cradle with T-handle

You will need :

28g (1oz) No.3 (2mm) cane.
85g (3oz) No.6 (2.6mm) cane.
56g (2oz) No.8 (3mm) cane.
No.10 (3.35mm) cane, 1.85m (2yd) long – for the base sticks.
No.2 (1.85mm) chair seating cane, 1m (1yd) long – optional for wrapping the base sticks.
No.6 (2.6mm) chair seating cane, 5.5m (6yd) long – for handle wrapping.
8mm ($\frac{5}{16}$ in) handle cane, 1.22m (48in) long.
Handle liners, 3.
All-purpose adhesive.
1 small nail.
Side-cutters.
Bodkin.
Round-nosed pliers.

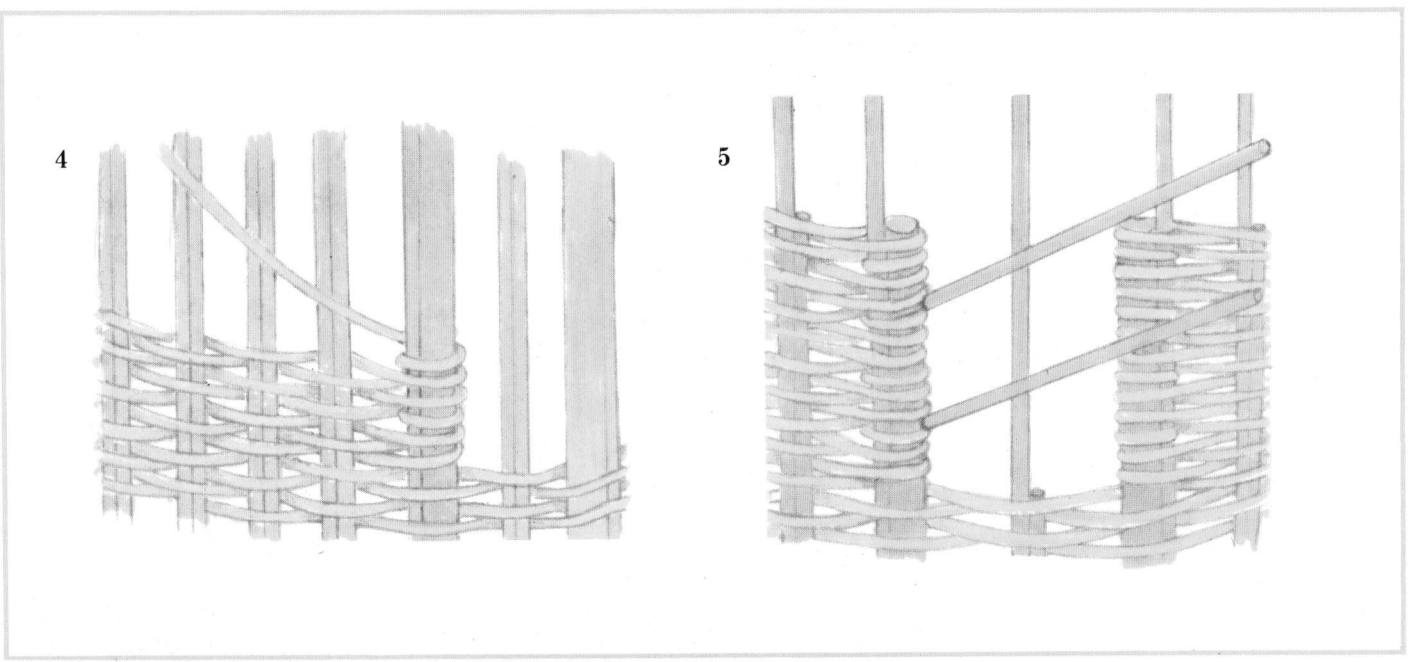

4. *Packing the front to form the lip
with a recess for the bottle's neck.*
5. *Additional stakes are inserted
for the border.*

*Left: A view of the wine cradle
showing the recess.*

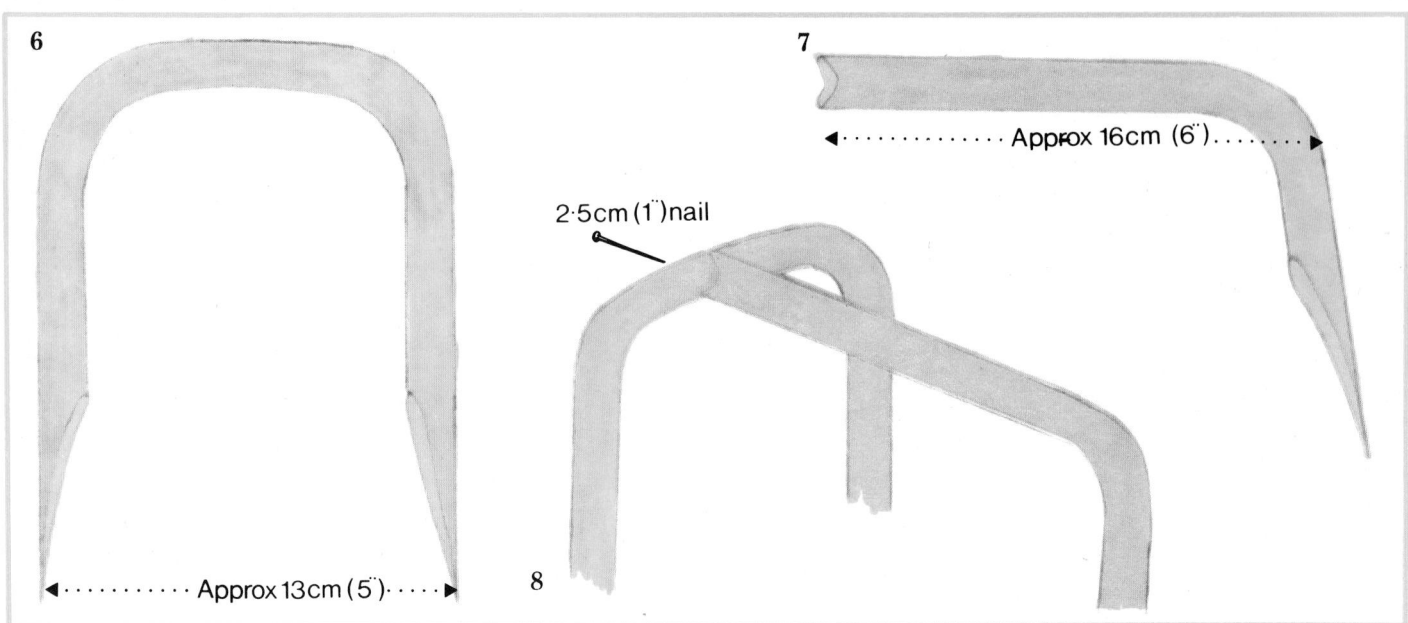

6. *Slype cuts on shaped handle form the cross-piece.*
7. *Slype and wedge cut on the handle cane.*
8. *Handle is assembled and then secured with a nail.*

Starting towards the back put on a plait [braid] border all the way around the cradle, over the edge of the thick sticks, down the side of the gap and up the opposite side. Now do the handles.

Handles Cut two pieces of 8mm ($\frac{5}{16}$in) handle cane, one 30cm (12in) long and the other 52cm (20in) long. Slype both ends of the longer piece and bend it into a U-shape with a flat bottom (fig.6). Remove the handle liners along the sides and insert the handle cane. Slype one end of the shorter piece of handle cane and bend the cane 15cm (6in) from the pointed end (fig.7). Remove the handle liner at the back and insert the slyped end of the handle cane so that it is leaning towards the other handle cane. Cut a wedge into the forward end of the handle so that it fits snugly into the cane of the cross handle. Leave these handles in this position to dry. Stick the wedge-cut to the cross handle and nail through the cross handle so that the nail passes into end of the other part of handle (fig.8).

Using No.6 (2.6mm) chair seating cane wrap the handle by starting at the back with the usual cross and leader. When you are 2.5cm (1in) from the cross handle take the leader right over the top and around to the underside. Continue wrapping so that the end of the leader is also bound in. Peg the end of the wrapping cane, which will be bound in later. Wrap the cross handle in the usual way, using a leader as before. When you reach the centre bind in the wrapping cane from the other part of the handle. Criss-cross the wrapping over at this point so that the handle cane is completely covered. Keep the pattern of the leader the same as for the other side and finish off. Peg all three ends of handle under waling.

Starting square work

Square work is the most difficult regular-shaped basketry to do. It is worked very differently from other shapes which have some sticks threaded through others to start the base. To start square work the base is not made with a criss-cross pattern of sticks as in round or oval work. The terms square work or square basketry are used loosely as they denote baskets which have corners and are usually rectangular – very few baskets are ever really square.

Flat square work To begin square basketry start practising by making flat bases. Two small square 'mats' will make a needlecase or a notebook cover. With more experience you can make binder covers for recipes and magazines, a cover for a scrapbook or use six square bases as a set of place mats. Working on a larger scale you can make window shutters and a headboard for a bed as shown in the next chapter. But start first on something small.

A screwblock is used to start square work. Screwblocks can be bought from crafts stores but these tend to be very light and small and only suitable for very light work. It is easy to make one at home and also inexpensive. The width of a square base is limited to the length of the screwblock. Normally 38cm (15in) is adequate but for larger items – for example a headboard – you would need a screwblock 66cm (26in) long.

Place the two pieces of wood together as shown in fig.1, and drill two holes 8cm (3in) from each end. The holes are drilled through two pieces to make sure that the holes correspond. Push the bolts through the holes and screw on the washers and wing nuts.

Using the screwblock To start a base the stakes are placed upright between the two parts of the screwblock. The wing nuts are then tightened to secure the stakes. The base sticks are cut to the length required plus 2.5cm-5cm (1in-2in) for clamping in the screwblock plus enough to trim the ends once the work is complete.

The size of the cane used, the number of base sticks and the distance between the sticks will vary according to the size and function of the finished article. Generally the sticks on each edge are thicker than those inside so that the edges are neat and firm. Sometimes these outer sticks are doubled to give a really strong base. If the

Screwblock
You will need : 2 softwood strips 5cm by 8cm (2in by 3in), 38cm (15in) long (or, for a larger screwblock, 2 pieces of softwood 8cm by 8cm (3in by 3in), 66cm (26in) long). Two 15cm (6in) coach bolts with a diameter of 6mm ($\frac{1}{4}$in). Wing nuts and washers to fit the bolt. These are suitable for both screwblocks. Hand drill and bit large enough to drill holes for the coach bolts.

Below: Measurements for making a screwblock.

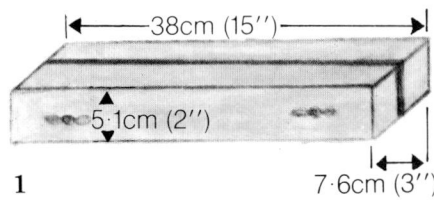

1

outer sticks are thicker than the inner ones they won't fit into the screwblock without some preparation. The thicker sticks need to be cut down so that the part that is clamped in the screwblock is the same thickness as the smaller sticks. Make two cuts about 2.5cm (1in) from the end of each of the thicker sticks (fig.2). Try to make the cuts as square as possible and not tapered. The sticks are now ready for use with the screwblock.

Remember that the larger the article the thicker the cane must be and the number of sticks must also be increased. The distance between the sticks will determine the distance between the side stakes later, so don't have them too far apart. For small items place the sticks 12mm-18mm ($\frac{1}{2}$in-$\frac{3}{4}$in) apart and for medium-sized items 2.5cm-3cm (1in-1$\frac{1}{4}$in) apart.

Needlecase

The cover consists of two bases each measuring about 8.5cm by 13cm (3$\frac{1}{4}$in by 5in) and could equally well be used to cover a notebook. This will give you the necessary experience to embark on a larger project. As the materials used are small in quantity, there is little waste if the results are not entirely satisfactory.

Cut two sticks of No.12 (3.75mm) cane, four sticks of No.6 (2.6mm) cane – all 18cm (7in) long. Trim one end of each of the thick sticks (fig.2). Place these two sticks in the screwblock 8cm (3in) apart – measure from the centre of one stick to the centre of the other. Place four thinner sticks between the two sticks in the screwblock. Space them evenly and keep them upright. Tighten the screwblock so that all the sticks are held firmly in position. You

2. The thick outer sticks are trimmed to the same thickness as the cane used for the inner sticks.
3. Start needlecase cover with one row of pairing.
4. Extra twists on the outer sticks prevent gaps showing.

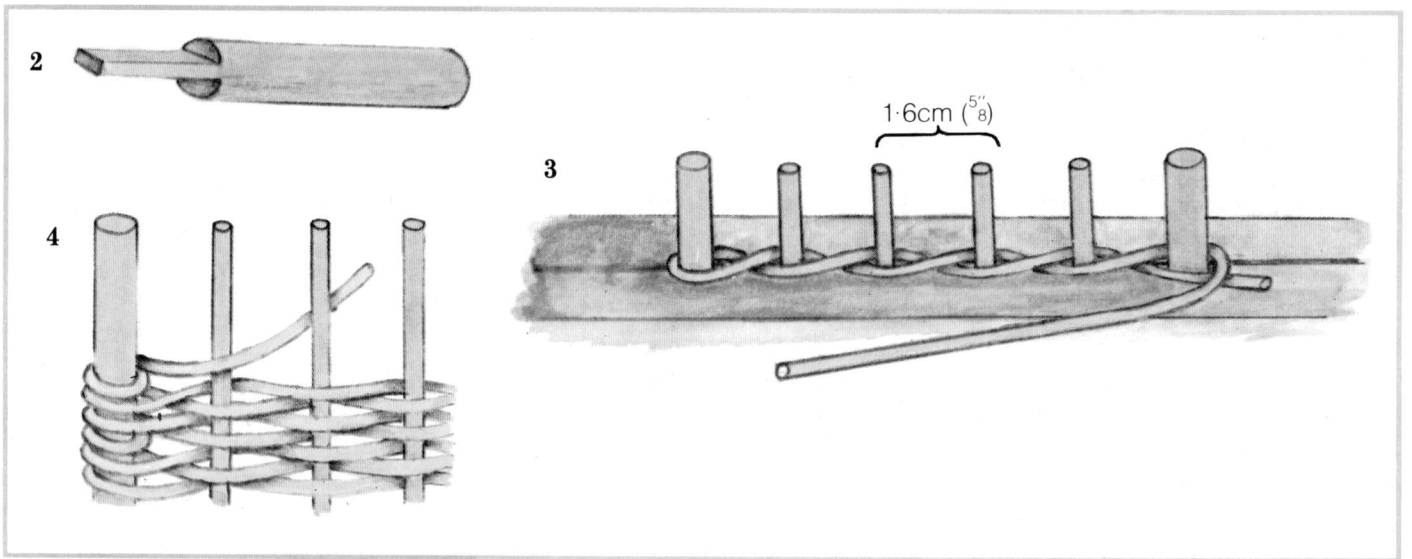

1·6cm ($\frac{5}{8}$'')

Needlecase
You will need :
28g (1oz) No.3 (2mm) cane.
140cm (56in) No.6 (2.6mm) cane.
70cm (28in) No.12 (3.75mm) cane.
4 small nails.
2 binder rings 18mm (¾in)
diameter – available from
stationers.
Felt to fit inside cover.
No.2 (1.85mm) chair seating cane
1.85m (2yd) long, or narrow
enamelled wrapping cane –
optional.
Screwblock.
Side-cutters.
Bodkin.
Round-nosed pliers.

Left: The borders of the needle-case are whipped with enamelled wrapping cane to secure them to the base. Binder rings are used to assemble the case with a piece of felt stitched between.

may have cut the outer ones too much or too little so that they, or the inner ones, wobble about. If so, adjust them or cut new ones – you cannot make a good base unless all the sticks are firmly held. Although a square base is mainly randed, the first row is paired and the last row is mock paired. Take a length of No.3 (2mm) cane and loop it around the left hand outer stick so that you have a long end and a short end of 20cm (8in). Use these two weavers and pair to the other end of the line of sticks (fig.3).

Drop the short end and continue with the long end only. Take it around the right-hand outer stick and then rand back to the left. Continue to rand backwards and forwards but on every other round the weaver must be taken around the outside sticks twice. This is because as you rand backwards and forwards you pass twice over the centre sticks while going around each outer stick once only. The extra twist will prevent any grins (gaps) appearing along the thick sticks (fig.4). If the randing is packed down you will need

5. Mock pairing completes the
base weaving.
6. Three stakes to the front
starts the border.
7. Stakes 1 and 3 form
the first pair.
8. Three pairs at the front.

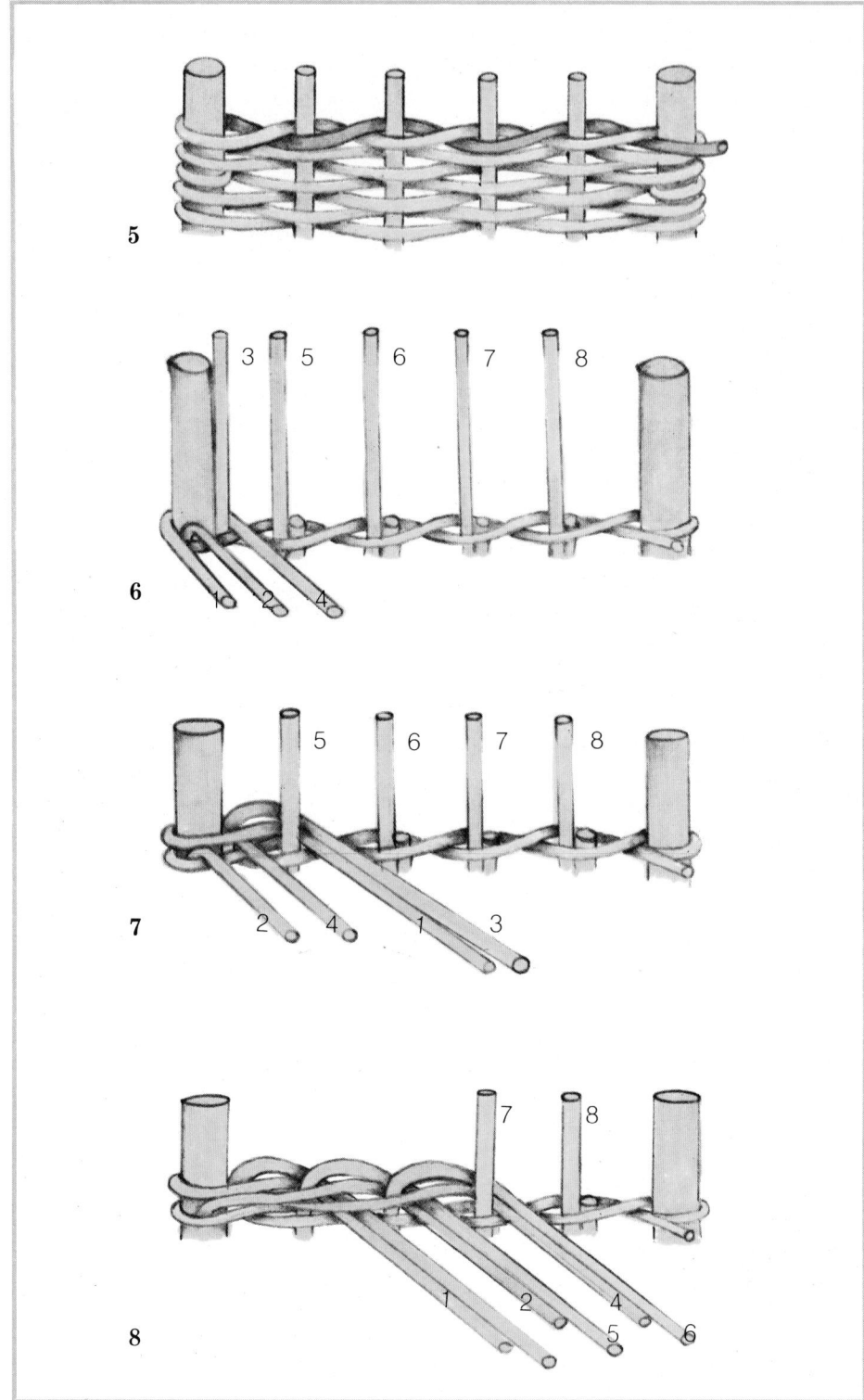

less double twists – adjust the wraps around the outer sticks as you work to cover the sticks but try to be constant, ie an extra wrap on every second or third round at regular intervals.

Measure the width of the work as you go along to make sure that the canes do not slope inwards or outwards. It is very important when doing square work to see that the sticks remain upright and parallel. Measure as you progress and don't let the sticks lean backwards or forwards or they will end up distorted.

Joining new weavers is done exactly as for round and oval work. Make sure that the ends always lie at the back of the work.

Continue randing until the work measures 11.5cm (4½in) in height. There should still be a short length of the sticks showing beyond the randing. This is for the last row which is mock pairing.

Mock pairing End the randing so that the weaver is on the left side of the work and has passed around the outer stick. Mock pair by taking the weaver in front of one stick and behind one stick, but each time it comes to the front, thread it underneath the weaver of the previous row. It should look just like pairing (fig.5). Continue all the way across to the end until the weaver reaches the right hand outer stick. Remove the work from the screwblock and trim all the weaver ends but do not cut any of the surplus stick ends yet. Replace the work in the screwblock and tighten it.

Three-rod border for square work Cut six stakes 13cm (5in) long and one piece 20cm (8in) long, all from No.3 (2mm) cane. Trim the surplus stick ends of the inner sticks only and place the screwblock and work so that the wrong side of the work faces you.

Insert one border stake into the weaving beside and to the left of each of the inner sticks. In this case (because the work is so small) insert the stakes about 2.5cm (1in) into the weaving. Insert one border stake down the side of the left outer stick. Using a bodkin to help you, insert one border stake into the weaving in front of the left outer stick and bend this down to the front of the work.

Loop the 20cm (8in) border stake in the middle and wrap it around the outer left hand stick and the border stake next to it (fig.6). You should now have three stakes to the front and five standing upright. The three stakes to the front represent the first three stakes that are bent down to start a normal three-rod border.

Take stake 1 and pass it in front of the outer stick and stake 3 and behind stake 5 and back to the front (fig.7). Bend stake 3 down to lie behind and beside stake 1. Take stake 2 in front of stake 5 and behind stake 6 and back to the front. Bend stake 5 to lie behind and beside stake 2. Take stake 4 in front of stake 6 and behind stake 7 and back to the front. Bend stake 6 down to lie behind and beside stake 4. You will now have three pairs to the front (fig.8)

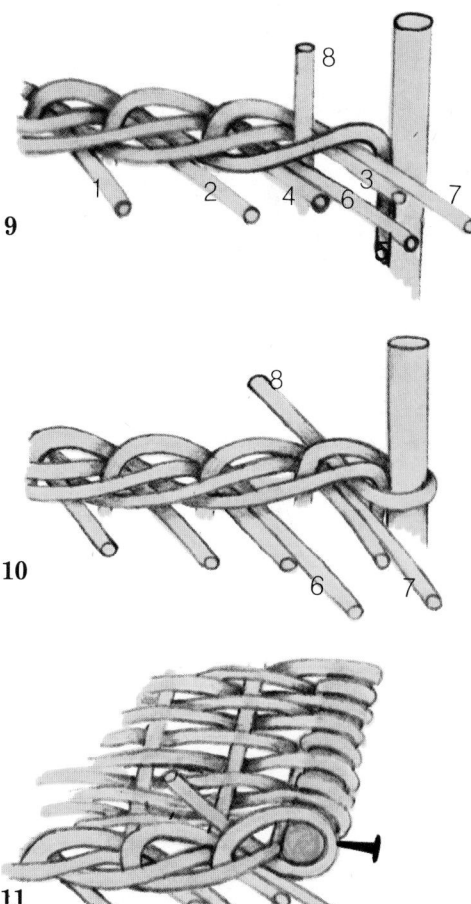

9. First stage in finishing the border.
10. Stake eight ends at back.
11. Nail secures border to outer thick stick.

On a larger edge you would continue with a three-rod border in the usual way but for this small base there is room for only one more stake. Take the fifth stake from the right in front of stake 7 and behind stake 8 and back to the front. Bend down stake 7 from last pair. You are now ready to finish the border.

To finish the border Take stake 3, the longer one of the pair, in front of stake 8 and up to the right hand outer stick. Nip this border stake so that it will bend down just before the outer stick. Cut it off about 4cm (1½in) below the nip and point the end. Push the pointed end into the weaving beside the outer stick (fig.9).

Bend down stake 8 (the last one) and pass it behind the right around the outer stick and thread it under the bent down stake (the last one you used) from the front to the back (fig.10). This stake can be left there so trim it neatly or it can be threaded through the work once more so that it lies on the same side as all the other ends – which is the back of the work. In this way others are invisible.

Secure the border by hammering a small nail into the border stakes that went around the two outer sticks, and into the outer sticks (fig.11). Put the same three-rod border on the other edge. Start with the wrong side of the work facing you. Cut off the protruding outer sticks close to the border and trim off surplus border stake ends with the side cutters.

Whipping The border can be secured further by binding it in one or two places with fine chair seating cane. This is known as whipping. The method is as follows:

Insert the cane into the weaving about 18mm (¾in) down from the border between two stakes. Use the long end to bind over the border and back through the randing at the same place seven times. Wrap the short end in as you work. Try to make the whipping fan out over the border but keep it in the same place in the randing. Secure the end by looping it once or twice through the whipping at the back and then weave it away.

Work another base in exactly the same way for the other cover taking great care to keep them both the same size. Put two binder rings through the weaving on one side of the covers and cut felt to fit. Make holes to coincide with the rings and insert between covers.

Magazine cover

Two bases measuring 23cm by 32cm (9in by 13in) are joined with two binder rings to form the cover.

Cut two sticks of 10mm handle cane 38cm (15in) long, and six sticks of No.15 (4.5mm) cane 38cm (15in) long. Cut one end of each of the two thick sticks to fit into the screwblock so that the two

---

Magazine cover

You will need :
170g (6oz) No.6 (2.6mm) cane.
No.15 (4.5mm) cane 3.66m (4yd) long.
10mm handle cane 1.85m (2yd) long.
4 small nails.
3 binder rings.
No.4 (2.25mm) chair seating cane or wrapping cane 3.66m (4yd) long – optional.
Screwblock.
Side-cutters.
Bodkin.
Round-nosed pliers.

outer ones – centre to centre – are 23cm (9in) apart and space the inner sticks evenly, as you did for the needlecase.

Using No.6 (2.6mm) cane put on one row of pairing. Rand for 31cm (12¼in) and put on one row of mock pairing. Using No.6 (2.6mm) cane border down as for the previous cover. You will need nine stakes 20cm (8in) long and one to loop around the outer stick 38cm (15in) long. Pin the border down with small nails and whip with chair seating cane if you wish.

Repeat the above to make the second cover.

Insert binder rings to complete.

You could also use the cover for a photograph album.

Above: The completed binder cover showing the attractive whipped borders.

Patterns in square work

The headboard

The headboard is 91.5cm (36in) wide and 52cm (20in) high. It can be used to replace an existing headboard or you can attach it to the wall by hooks secured to the wall with wall plugs and positioned to hook round the sticks where the coil pattern starts.

Working with such thick sticks can be awkward so do not attempt it until you have some experience with square work.

Cut the two thick sticks so that the ends fit into the screwblock with the nine inner sticks. Place the thick sticks so that they are 48cm (19in) apart – centre to centre – and space the other sticks evenly between them as you have done in previous projects.

Weave with well-soaked No.8 (3mm) cane starting with one row of pairing and continue to rand backwards and forwards for 16.5cm (6½in). Cut the third inner stick from the left level with the randing. Insert one length of No.15 (4.5mm) cane (it must be at least 3m (3yd) long) into the weaving just to the left of the fourth inner stick from the left. Coil this piece around and around for about 55cm (22in) and secure it with adhesive tape against the two sticks. Leave enough space after the last coil to allow you to put on 16.5cm (6½in) of randing and a row of mock pairing. Rand backwards and forwards on the first three sticks on the left only for 61cm (2in) catching in the coil when convenient.

Cut the third inner stick from the right and place a length of No. 15 (4.5mm) cane against the second inner stake from the right. Repeat the coiling as before and end it 8cm (3in) short of the previous coils. Rand backwards and forwards on the three inner sticks and then on the three right-hand sticks, catching in the coils as you work. Rand to the end of the second length of coil.

You now have to replace the cut stick. Measure the length you need from the end of the coil to the end of the other sticks and add on an additional piece before cutting. Use adhesive tape to keep it in position against the coils until there is enough randing to hold it securely. Remove adhesive tape and pull the stick up so that the end is butting up to the last coil. Rand backwards and forwards to the first coil and catch it in where convenient. At the same time

Headboard
You will need : 677g (1½lb) No.8 (3mm) cane. No.15 (4.5mm) cane, 5.5m (6yd) long. 9 lengths of 8mm handle cane, 102cm (40in) long or 9 lengths of dowelling – 6mm (¼in) diameter – 102cm (40in) long. 2 lengths of dowelling – 18mm (¾in) diameter – 102cm (40in) long. 12 small nails. Screwblock – at least 66cm (26in) long. Adhesive tape. Side-cutters. Bodkin. Round-nosed pliers.

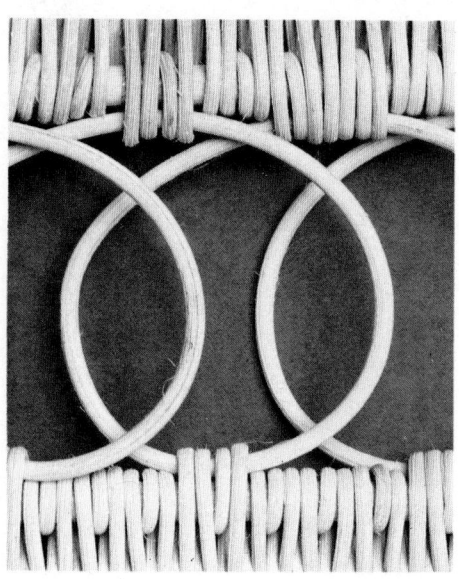

bind in the end of the coil cane. Replace the other missing stick in the same way and rand right across for a further 16.5cm (6½in). Finish with one row of mock pairing.

The border is put on in the same way as before but insert one stake on each side of each stick otherwise the border will be too loose. You will therefore need 20 stakes 25cm (10in) long and one longer piece 52cm (20in) long all of No.8 (3mm) cane, for each end. Try to keep these border stakes inserted to the same depth all the way along. Nip them down and put the border on as before. Nail the four small nails into the corners and put in a nail through the end of each coil into the adjoining stick to keep the coils steady. Secure the headboard to the wall with hooks.

Above: Headboard made on a large size screwblock.

Opposite: Detail of coil pattern on headboard.

63

Upsett work

After you have mastered the technique of flat square work, you can build up square baskets suitable for sewing boxes, picnic hampers and wine baskets, etc. The instructions in this chapter make it possible for you to combine techniques and designs so that you can adapt the baskets to your own needs.

The techniques include upsetting, fastenings, hinges, small handles and rib randing. The techniques used for making the lid and hinges are suitable for other shapes such as oval and round work, and the small handles can be put onto any basket where you do not require a large handle. We show you how to make the bottle tote first.

Bottle tote

Start with this basket as it is easier than the basket with the lid. The basket measures 20cm by 30cm (8in by 11¾in), and is 20cm (8in) high excluding the handle. The basket is roomy and strong enough to hold six bottles without overcrowding.

For the base cut the 8mm handle cane into seven pieces, each 30cm (12in) long. Split three of these right down the centre along the length. They will split easily if you make a small cut with a trimming knife, and then pull them apart with your fingers. Five of the split handle canes will form the inner sticks of the base – the sixth piece is discarded. Now prepare your screwblock.

Set the sticks up in the screwblock with double whole canes on the outsides. The distance between the outer sticks must be 18cm (7in) – centre to centre. Trim the outer sticks to fit into the block with inner sticks. Set the split canes up so that they are evenly spaced between the outer sticks. Let the curved side of the split canes face you as you proceed with your weaving.

Weaving with No.5 (2.5mm) cane put on one row of pairing, then rand and finish off with one row of mock pairing so that the base is 27cm (10½in) high. Remember to twist the weaver around the outer stick on every second or third round to avoid grins (gaps) showing. Keep the sticks upright and do not let the work get wider or narrower towards the top.

Remove the base from the screwblock and trim the ends of the weavers and the four ends of the outer sticks – *do not trim the inner sticks for the time being.*

For the stake up cut 21 stakes 45cm (18in) long and 14 stakes 52cm (20in) long, all from No.10 (3.35mm) cane. Point the 21 shorter ones at one end with a short point and the others with the

Left: Full instructions are given to show you how to make these super baskets. Ideal for picnics, one is designed for carrying food, and the other carries bottles.

usual longer point. There are 14 of these.

Place the base flat on the table with the trimmed ends upwards. This will become the inside of the basket. Use the bodkin to form a channel and insert one of the longer stakes into the base between the outer sticks of one corner. It does not matter if the stake lies underneath the two sticks in the crevice that is formed by the roundness of the canes. Repeat with another stake at the other end along the length. Now you are ready to stake up.

Stake up along the length. Eleven of the shorter stakes must be inserted into one side along the length of the work. Use a pencil and make marks 6mm ($\frac{1}{4}$in) in from the corners. Make nine more marks, evenly spaced between the two outside marks.

Use the bodkin to make holes through both the outer sticks in which to insert the stakes. Start at one end and insert each stake as you go along. Push the bodkin into the outer sticks from the outside and in between the weaving canes where the marks are. Make the holes quite large. Most difficulties encountered in staking up square work are caused by holes which are not large enough. Pull the bodkin out and insert the stake immediately. The hole closes up quickly when the bodkin is removed, so if you were not quick enough open the hole again with the bodkin and try again.

Insert the stake until you can see the point on the inside of the outer sticks. Make sure that all the pointed section is inside the sticks – if it is not the stake will crack and split on the upsett.

Now repeat on the opposite side. Insert two long stakes between the outer sticks (as before). Instead of eleven stakes along the length, ten stakes are inserted to create an odd number which makes randing easier for you to work with.

Cut off any surplus ends from the inner sticks and insert one of the long stakes beside each stick at each end. It doesn't matter which side of the stick they are inserted but try to space them evenly.

For the upsett make sure that the stakes are well soaked and nip each one close to the base. Bend them all up together and tie tightly. If you have not trimmed all the outer base sticks, do so now.

Insert four weavers of No.6 (2.6mm) cane into base and four-rod wale for four rounds. Keep corner stakes close together do not try to space them evenly – the closer together they are, the squarer the corners will be. Keep the waling upright.

Cut eight bye-stakes 20cm (8in) long, of No.15 (4.5mm) cane. Point one end of each and insert them into the waling – insert two bye-stakes at each corner, next to a stake on the side closest to the corner. The thicker bye-stakes are used to make the corners stronger and also help to keep the corners square.

Cut 27 bye-stakes 20cm (8in) long, of No.10 (3.35mm) cane and

Above: Well-soaked pieces of cane are twisted to form the partitions for the bottles.

insert them into the waling beside and to the right of the remaining stakes. Rand with No.6 (2.6mm) cane keeping the work straight up and the corners as square as possible. Continue until the randing measures 7cm (2¾in) in height.

Put on three rounds of waling using No.6 (2.6mm) cane. Insert the handle liners in the centre of the two short sides.

Rib randing is a decorative variation of randing. It is done by passing the cane in front of two stakes and behind one (instead of in front of one and behind one). This makes a thicker weave with a slight spiral effect. You have to have a number of stakes that will not divide by three or the weaver will go in front of the same stakes each time. Rib rand for 5cm (2in) with No.6 (2.6mm) cane. Wale with No.6 (2.6mm) cane for three rounds.

For the partitions cut a piece of well soaked No.8 (3mm) cane twice the width of the basket plus 30cm (12in). Bend it in the middle and loop it over a stake one third of the way down along the length. Twist the two ends together, quite tightly, until the twisted length is sufficient to reach across to the other side. Loop the two ends around a corresponding stake on the other side, one end going around one way and the other, the other way around. Weave the ends away on top of the waling. Repeat with a second piece of cane two thirds of the way along the length so that there are three equal partitions in the basket.

Cut a piece of No.8 (3mm) cane, twice the length of the basket, plus 30cm (12in). Bend it in the middle and loop it over one of the handle liners and its adjoining stake. Twist the ends together until it reaches the first of the cross partitions. Pass one cane around it as before. Twist again until you reach the other end and finish as before. You now have six equal partitions.

Trim the surplus ends of the bye-stakes, re-soak the stakes if necessary and nip them 6mm (¼in) above the waling. Put on a four-rod border. Try to keep the corners very square. Trim all the surplus ends so that none of them are protruding.

Point each end of the 10mm handle cane and shape the handle into a flat U-shape. Remove the liners and insert the handle well down into the work. You are now ready to rope the handle.

Cut 12 pieces of No.6 (2.6mm) cane, 102cm (40in) long. Insert six to the left of each end of the handle. Rope the handle and finish with a herringbone pattern for decoration.

Bottle tote
You will need : 56g (2oz) No.5 (2.5mm) cane. 170g (6oz) No.6 (2.6mm) cane. 113g (4oz) No.10 (3.35mm) cane. No.15 (4.5mm) cane, 1.83m (ft) long. No.8 (3mm) cane, 2.44m (8ft) long. 10mm handle cane, 90cm (3ft) long – use Malacca cane if you can obtain it. 8mm handle cane, 2.14m (7ft) long. 2 handle liners. Screwblock. Side-cutters. Bodkin. Round-nosed pliers.

Picnic hamper with lid

The outside measurements of the hamper are 38cm by 25cm (15in by 10in) height 14cm (5½in). The lid is secured with hinges and fasteners which can also be used on smaller items.

Picnic hamper with lid

You will need:
170g (6oz) No.5 (2.5mm) cane.
170g (6oz) No.6 (2.6mm) cane.
170g (6oz) No.10 (3.35mm) cane.
113g (4oz) No.15 (4.5mm) cane.
No.8 (3mm) cane. 3m (3yd) long.
No.4 (2mm) chair seating cane,
7.5m (8yd) long.
8mm handle cane 4.6m (5yd) long.
4 small nails.
All-purpose adhesive.
Screwblock.
Side-cutters.
Bodkin.
Round-nosed pliers.

Opposite: Techniques used to make the picnic hamper.
1. Diagonal cuts are made to fit.
2. Wedges are cut in the cane before it is bent.
3. Template for lid with the marks for the hinges.
4. Recesses cut to allow for the hinges.
5. Sticks inserted to position the pairing.

Small D-shaped handle – make this first so that it is ready when the time comes to fix it on. Cut a piece of 8mm handle cane 35cm (14in) long. Soak it well and bend it into a U-shape. Nip it hard with the round-nosed pliers 10cm (4in) in from each end. These 10cm (4in) sections form the straight side of the handle and each piece must be shaved away with a diagonal cut so that they form one thickness when put together (fig.1). If the ends will not come round far enough cut out a wedge shape where you nipped the cane (fig.2). This makes the cane more flexible.

Tie the handle together in its correct shape and leave it to dry. Glue the ends together and again tie in position and leave to dry.

Wrap the handle with chair seating cane. Start at the back of the handle which is the straight side – start and finish as for the handle on the wine cradle. The corners are difficult to keep tidy – wrap tightly and just do your best. You may use a leader on the curved side and, if you join it in before the corners, it will help to cover the corners and make them look more compact.

For the base cut four outer sticks of 8mm handle cane and 16 inner sticks (these are not split) of No.15 (4.5mm) cane – all 41cm (16in) long. Set them up in the screwblock with the handle cane on the outside and 23cm (9in) apart. Space the other sticks evenly.

Make the base as before – one row of pairing to start, then rand and finish with one row of mock pairing when the work measures 33cm (13½in) – all with No.5 (2.5mm) cane. Using No.10 (3.35mm) cane, cut 27 stakes 35cm (14in) long and 20 stakes 41cm (16in) long.

Stake up as before with the shorter stakes along the length and the long stakes into the ends. Nip the stakes and tie them up into two bunches – one at each end. This will prevent the base from becoming distorted and curling up.

Upsett with one row of four-rod waling and three rows of three-rod waling with No.6 (2.6mm) cane. Now prepare the bye-stakes.

Cut 39 bye-stakes of No.10 (3.35mm) and eight of No.15 (4.5mm) cane for the corners – all 13cm (5in) long. Insert them as before. Rand for 5cm (2in) with No.6 (2.6mm) cane.

To fix the handle mark its position in the centre of the long side you prefer. Select two stakes, one at each end of the flat side of the handle, which are convenient to carry the loops that will secure the handle. Now you are ready to prepare the loops.

Cut two pieces No.8 (3mm) cane, 35cm (14in) long. Make sure that they are well soaked and not brittle. Bend one in the middle and loop it around one of the selected stakes about 18mm (¾in) down from the top of the randing. Twist this cane for 18mm (¾in) by taking one end in each hand and crossing your hands over. Transfer the canes into the other hands and repeat for the required

68

length. This method produces a tight, even twist.

Place the handle in position so that the twist comes through the inside of the handle. Take the two ends of the twist upwards and loop them around the back of the same stake over the top of the randing. Weave the two ends away. Do not make the twist too loose nor too tight. It it is loose the handle will have too much play and if it is tight it will chafe the loops. Repeat with another loop at the other end of the handle.

Rand with No.6 (2.6mm) cane right around the basket. Continue until the randing measures 8cm (3in). Wale with No.6 (2.6mm) cane for four rounds. Put on a three-rod border and a follow-on trac border. Now you are ready to make the lid.

The lid If you have made your basket absolutely perfect the lid will be exactly the same shape as the base and slightly larger to allow for the upsett. However, as the shape is never constant, the lid must be made to fit the shape at the top of the basket.

A template is made by turning the basket upside down and placing it on a sheet of card. Draw all the way around the basket. This is to be the shape of the lid. Cut the template out to enable you to follow it closely (fig.3). This will form the pattern.

Mark the position of the hinges on the template along the length on the side opposite the handle. Cut 6mm (¼in) from the short sides of the template to allow for the borders.

Cut four sticks of 8mm handle cane and 16 of No.15 (4.5mm) cane – all the length of the template plus 5cm (2in). The extra 5cm (2in) is to allow for 2.5cm (1in) which goes into the screwblock and 2.5cm (1in) at the top end to make finishing easier.

Mark the outer stick along the side where the hinges are to be. Don't forget to allow for the extra length of the sticks. At the hinge marks cut haltway through the thickness of the cane so that the cuts are 18mm (¾in) long (fig.4).

Set the sticks in the screwblock to fit the template with the hinge cuts positioned as illustrated. Allow for the thickness of the weaving cane on each side. A stick with the hinge recesses must be on the inside with the recesses of both sticks matching (fig.5). Check that the sticks match up with the template.

Using No.5 (2.5mm) cane put on a row of pairing then, if the corners of the template are rounded, lift the pairing up to match the template. Place pieces of cane below the pairing to keep it in position and to pad the corners (fig.5).

Using No.6 (2.6mm) cane continue randing but fill up the hollow between the corners by weaving backwards and forwards until the weaving is straight all the way across. Continue randing and do not forget to pass the weaver twice around the outer stick on every

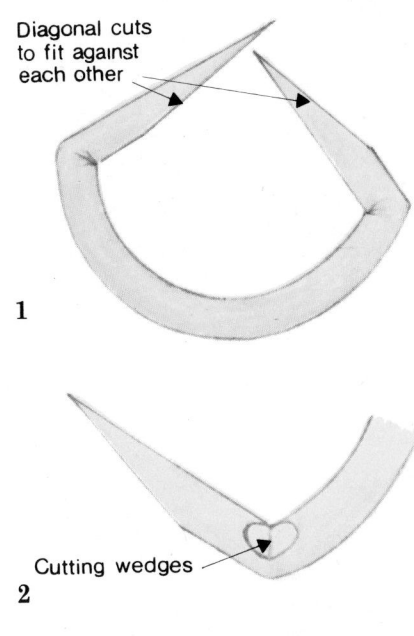

Diagonal cuts to fit against each other

1

Cutting wedges

2

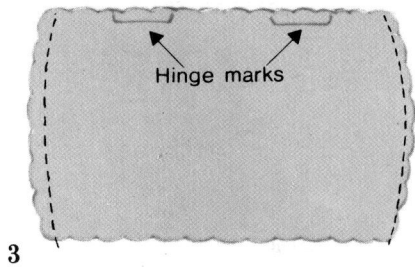

Hinge marks

3

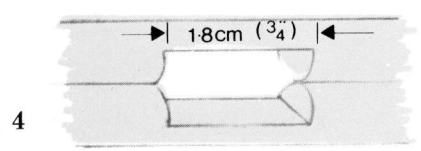

1·8cm (¾")

4

5

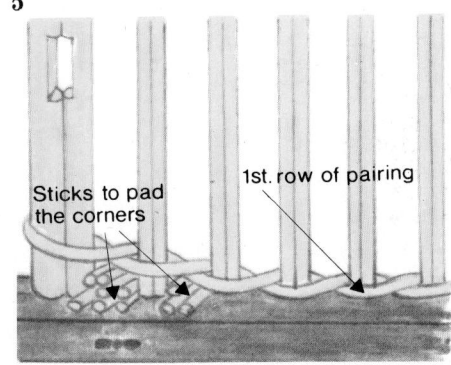

Sticks to pad the corners

1st. row of pairing

6

Top: Detail of D-shaped handle and the hasp and loop used to secure the basket lid. Above: Cane twisted together to form the hasp.

Opposite: Weaving with templates made from cardboard.

second or third round, until you reach the first hinge mark.

Continue to rand backwards and forwards but pass the cane around the inner of the two outside sticks so that the weaver settles into the cut-away part. When the end of the hinge mark is reached reverse back to passing right around the outer sticks.

Follow the template to the outer hinge and repeat the method of making the hinge space. Continue to the end of the lid. Pack again (weaving backwards and forwards going to one stake less each time) if necessary to make the rounded shape of the template. Finish with one row right across and put on one row of mock pairing. Complete lid with a three-rod border at each end and whip the borders with chair seating cane. Secure the border with small nails. Now you can prepare the hinges.

The hinges on baskets are very simple. Take a length of No.5 (2.5mm) cane (or chair seating cane) and insert it into the basket just under the border. Leave 23cm (9in) free on the inside (which will be woven away). Take the long end up and over the outer stick of the lid, through the hinge recess, down inside the lid and basket under the border so that it lies side by side with the other end. Continue doing this, over and over, until the hinge recess is filled up. Weave both ends away in the waling of the basket. Repeat the same procedure with the other hinge.

Fastenings – make two loops in the front of the basket, using No.8 (3mm) cane, in exactly the same way as for the loops that hold the handle. Select two suitable stakes, about 8cm (3in) in from each end. Start the loops about 18mm ($\frac{3}{4}$in) down from the waling and finish them just underneath the waling.

The hasps are similar or they may be braided instead. These are started and finished in the lid and drop down over the front and around the loops. Loop a piece of No.8 (3mm) cane around the first inner sticks from the front edge of the lid, and slightly to the left side of the loop in the basket.

Add a third cane for a braid. Twist (or braid) until there is sufficient length to go right around the loop on the opposite side from which you started and back up to meet the twist (or braid) again (fig.6). Here it crosses over itself – take one end of the cane through the twist (or braid) – and continue until you reach the first inner stick again, this time slightly to the right. Weave the ends away and repeat the same process on the other side.

Fasten the basket with a stick made from handle cane. Cut a piece long enough to pass through both loops with 5cm (2in) to overlap at both ends. Point one end. The other end may be left plain or make a loop of No.15 (4.5mm) cane, shaped and glued in place, and then wrapped over with chair seating cane.

Lampshades and templates

Basketry lampshades give a warm, attractive light and seem to suit most types of houses and cottages, but they are expensive to buy. However they are quite easy and inexpensive to make as they use very little cane and are well worth the effort.

This type of lampshade is open at both ends so the stakes are initially held in position in holes made in a cardboard disc. A wire ring with a bulb fitting must be inserted in the lampshade. In other words the lampshade is made to measure after a suitable lampshade ring has been selected. The rings are available in a wide range of sizes and shapes and are suitable for all types of light fittings.

Cylindrical shade

Start with a cylindrical shade, ie straight-sided with a circular cross-section with the same diameter throughout. The shade illustrated was made on a 23cm (9in) ring with a flat fitting and is 20cm (8in) high. It looks lovely on a pottery base.

Place the lampshade ring on the cardboard and draw around it with pencil. Mark the pencil ring at approximately 2.5cm (1in) intervals all the way around. There should be about 29 marks but, whatever the number, make sure that it will not divide by three otherwise you will not be able to rib rand. If necessary, alter the number of marks to adjust this. Bind the lampshade ring with the tape so that it is ready to insert at a later stage.

Pierce the cardboard with the bodkin at each of the marks just outside the pencilled ring. The holes should be just big enough to take the No.6 (2.6mm) cane. If the holes are too big the stakes will slip about too easily and will make the first process difficult. Cut one stake for each of the holes from No.6 (2.6mm) cane, 61cm (24in) long. Insert one stake into each hole and pull them through so that 20cm (8in) protrudes on one side for the first border. Nip the short ends near the cardboard so that they turn down easily without cracking or breaking into pieces.

The next step is putting on a border which will form either the top or bottom of the shade. If you put this border on in the usual way, ie from left to right, you will find that when you turn it up the other

---

Cylindrical lampshade

You will need :
Thick cardboard disc with 30cm (12in) diameter.
23cm (9in) diameter lampshade ring.
Lampshade tape – enough to cover the ring.
56g (2oz) No.6 (2.6mm) cane.
28g (1oz) No.5 (2.5mm) cane.
56g (2oz) flat cane – this is similar to the ordinary cane except that it is flat and only available in one size.
Needle and cotton to secure ring in position.
Side-cutters.
Bodkin.
Round-nosed pliers.

Left: The stakes for this lampshade are cut from round cane, and the weaving is done with flat cane.

way to start the weaving, the stakes will lean over to the right which makes it difficult to control them. This is avoided by putting down the border going the other way, ie from right to left.

Put on a three-rod border (fig.1) working right to left. You will find it easier if you rest the edge of the cardboard disc on a table with the long ends pointing towards you. Stand up and lean over the cardboard to manipulate the border canes. Do not trim the ends when you have finished the border.

When the border is complete turn the shade so that the cardboard is flat on the table. Place a weight inside the cardboard to keep it steady. Using No.5 (2.5mm) cane work five rounds of waling. Remember to step-up at the end of each round.

Cut two bye-stakes of No.6 (2.6mm) cane for each stake, all 20cm (8in) long. Point one end of each and insert them – one on each side of each stake – into the work. Rib rand (in front of two, behind one and back to the front) with flat cane for 14cm (5½in). Be very careful to keep the sides quite straight.

Wale with No.5 (2.5mm) cane for one round and insert the taped ring, which should fit exactly, continue with four more rows of waling. If you let the sides curve in or out and the ring will not fit, insert it from the other end of the work.

Nip the *stakes* 6mm (¼in) above the waling and cut off all the surplus ends of the *bye-stakes*. Put on a three-rod border in the normal way (left to right) and a follow-on trac border. Turn the shade the other way up to finish the first border.

If you are making a number of shades and want to re-use the cardboard disc, undo the border and gently pull the cardboard up and away from the stakes. Set the disc aside to dry. Turn the border down again (re-soak the stakes if necessary) and put on a follow-on trac border. Trim the ends. If you are making one shade only and do not need to re-use the cardboard disc, soak it in water to soften it and then pull it away from the shade. Put on a follow-on trac border and trim the ends.

Stitch the ring in place to hold it securely. Do not stitch through

Right: The shade is started with a three-rod border working from right to left.

1

74

the canes. Take the thread around the stakes only so that it is lost to sight between the small spaces in the waling.

Vase-shaped shade

The size of the shade is a matter of choice. The one illustrated was made with a 10cm (4in) lampshade ring and is 23cm (9in) high. Lampshades are always started in the same way. The shape of the shade will affect the distance between the stakes depending on how much it curves outwards. If you want the shade to come out a

Vase-shaped shade

You will need :
Thick cardboard disc with 15cm (6in) diameter.
10cm (4in) diameter lampshade ring covered with tape.
56g (2oz) No.6 (2.6mm) cane.
56g (2oz) No.4 (2.25mm) cane.
Needle and cotton to secure ring in position.
Side-cutters.
Bodkin.
Round-nosed pliers.

Left: Lampshades can be made in a variety of shapes. This one is vase-shaped, and is made with double randing. It is mounted on a lamp fitting without a base. It can also be used on a base, or as a hanging shade.

Right: Open-worked shades are quick to make and do not need much cane. The shade is worked from the smaller open end. The stakes and bye-stakes are bent outwards and held in place with a row of fitching.

great deal, the stakes around the ring will need to be much closer at the ring end so that they are not too far apart at the edge. Start this shade with the stakes 15mm ($\frac{5}{8}$in) apart to allow for the flow in the middle; 23 stakes were used for the lampshade illustrated. If you wish to rib rand, the number of stakes must not be divisible by three. To work a double rand any odd number is sufficient.

Cut the stakes 61cm (24in) long using No.6 (2.6mm) cane. Insert them into the cardboard disc and put on a border as for the previous lampshade. Put on four rounds of waling with No.4 (2.25mm) cane. Now you must prepare your bye-stakes.

Using No.6 (2.6mm) cane cut one bye-stake for each stake. Point one end of each and insert the pointed ends into the waling to the right of the stakes. Double rand with two weavers No. 4 (2.25mm) cane. Always keep one weaver on top of the other and do not let them twist around. Support the stakes with the thumb and fore-finger of the left hand. Try not to let the weavers dominate the stakes. Keep the sides of the stakes quite straight for 5cm (2in) then allow them to flow out to a diameter of 14cm (5½in). Try to make a 'bulb' shape. Decrease the diameter as you proceed to 10cm (4in).

Put on three rounds of waling with No.4 (2.25mm) cane. Trim bye-stakes and border down with a three-rod border and follow-on trac border. Remove the cardboard and finish the first border as for cylindrical lampshade. Trim the weaver ends and stitch in the ring to finish as for the cylindrical lampshade.

Open-worked shade

This shade is not covered with weaving. The stakes are left open in parts and held in position with a row of fitching. The light bulb can be hidden by covering the inside of shade with a suitable lamp-shade lining material – available from large departmental stores. The completed shade is 18cm (7in) high.

Make 21 holes round the pencilled ring on the cardboard as before. Cut 21 stakes 45cm (18in) long from No.6 (2.6mm) cane and insert them into the holes in the cardboard disc so that 10cm (4in) protrude from one side.

Put on a trac border – behind one, in front of three and tuck it to the inside in the next space – going from right to left. Turn the shade the other way up and put on four rounds of waling with No.4 (2.25mm) cane. Now prepare your bye-stakes.

Cut 42 bye-stakes of No.6 (2.6mm) cane 38cm (15in) long. Point them at one end and insert them into the waling – one on each side of each of the stakes. Nip these groups of three stakes so they will bend outwards. Put on one round of fitching 9cm (3½in) away from the waling to make the diameter of the shade 18cm (7in).

Wale for four rounds with No.4 (2.24mm) cane, continue to shape the work outwards. Put on a trac border (left to right) with all three stakes in turn – behind one, in front of three and tuck the canes to the inside in the next space.

Finish the first border as for the previous shades and trim all the ends. Shape and stitch lampshade lining material into the lamp-shade and stitch in the ring to finish.

Choosing the right base

Remember that your completed shade will need a pretty base. Try to choose one in a natural substance, such as stoneware or pottery, with an attractive glaze. A badly chosen base can ruin the effect of your work so think about it before you choose.

Open-work shade

You will need :
9cm (3½in) diameter lampshade ring covered with tape.
Thick cardboard disc with 12.5cm (5in) diameter.
Thread, needle.
56gm (2oz) No.6 (2.6mm) cane.
28gm (1oz) No.4 (2.25mm) cane.
25cm (¼yd) lampshade lining material – optional.
Side-cutters.
Bodkin.
Round-nosed pliers.

Cane chair seating

Caned chair seating dates back to ancient Egypt and, although nothing was written about the technique until this century, early artefacts such as Tutankhamun's day bed show that the method has changed very little. Caned furniture has been fashionable over the centuries, but especially during the past three hundred years. In the 18th century finer cane than was previously used became available in Europe, and elegant cane-bottomed chairs by cabinet makers, such as Adam and Hepplewhite, were the result.

Caning reached its greatest popularity in the 19th century with the development of bent-wood furniture, and in Vienna one factory produced 400,000 bent-wood chairs in a year. Bent-wood furniture is popular again and pieces which need re-caning can often be bought cheaply. For this reason, as well as the innate pleasure of working with cane, it is a craft worth pursuing. Do not be too ambitious in the early stages however – leave antique chairs alone until you become experienced at handling and weaving cane. Start with a square or oblong shape before attempting more complicated ones and use a cheap second-hand chair.

Materials

The materials required are readily available and apart from the cane very little else is required.

Chair seating cane comes from the same source as the cane used for weaving baskets. It is available in two qualities and various sizes. Blue tie is the best quality cane and is used for antique chairs, but red tie is suitable for most other chairs.

The cane is available in six sizes which are numbered from 1 to 6. The thinner the cane the smaller the number. Two different sizes of cane are often used on one chair; the most common sizes are No.2 and No.4. The size of the cane required depends on the distance between the holes on the chair frame. The usual distance between holes is 12mm ($\frac{1}{2}$in) making the frame suitable for the ever-popular seven-step pattern illustrated in the photograph.

If the holes in a frame are closer together than 12mm ($\frac{1}{2}$in) the cane will become crowded, making it difficult to work, and No.2 and No.3 must be used instead. For very fine work use No.1 and No.2. If you are re-caning a chair, take a sample if possible and purchase a similar-sized cane to the one used originally.

Although two sizes of cane are traditional, most people – for reasons of economy – will prefer to use only one size of cane (unless a large number of chairs are being re-caned). This is because one bundle of cane will be more than sufficient for caning one chair; working with different sizes will mean left-over material unless several chairs are being caned.

Opposite: Close-up photograph of chairs with their seats caned in the popular seven-step pattern.

Pegs are required for chair seating. They are used to hold the cane temporarily during the weaving although some are left permanently to secure odd ends or to plug 'blind' holes. Any pointed 5cm (2in) sticks are suitable, as is thick cane if you have it. Alternatives, for temporary pegs, are golf tees and Rawlplugs.

Tools

There can be few crafts that require less tools and most of the tools are part of any household, or can be improvised.

Scissors to cut the cane. Any size will do.

A Knife to cut the cane where the scissors cannot reach; can also be used to make and point the pegs.

A Clearer is used to clear the holes. An 8cm (3in) nail is suitable if the pointed end is cut off. Similarly a metal knitting needle or a screwdriver can be used – the diameter of the tool should not be more than 3mm ($\frac{1}{8}$in).

Bodkin A small fine bodkin is very useful to help the cane through tight spaces, but you can make do with a hat pin.

Small hammer for rapping the knots flat at the finish and for tapping the pegs into holes.

Preparing the chair

A chair must be stripped of all its old cane and any repairs to the frame must be done before re-caning is started. The frame must be sanded and varnished or painted, as this is not possible once the weaving is started. The old cane can be cut away close to the frame and kept for reference – this is especially useful if the shape is irregular. Alternatively, before removing the old cane make a sketch of the frame, marking the holes and the number of canes from each hole and their direction – this is particularly useful for round and oval shapes which are more complicated.

Remove all the old cane from the holes and underneath the seat. If the caning has been pegged, knock all the pegs out of the holes using the clearer. If the pegs are very stubborn and will not come out with gentle tapping, it is less strain on the frame if you drill a hole in the peg – use a drill bit the same size as the existing holes.

Sometimes corner holes are 'blind', ie they do not go right through the wood. In these cases the pegs must be drilled out to clear the original hole. Once all the old cane is stripped, the holes cleared and the frame painted or varnished, you can start weaving.

Seven-step pattern

If you are working on a square or oblong frame this pattern is simple and should present no difficulties.

Preparation The cane must be prepared before it is used. You will find it easy to handle the cane if you dip it in hot water for a moment before using it. Keep the cane wet while working by passing it through a bowl of water. The cane will also absorb enough water if you dip your fingers in the water and stroke the underside of the cane (not the glossy side) occasionally. While dry cane is very brittle, and cracks and splits easily, you should never soak the cane or it will become discoloured, nor should you wrap it up in a damp cloth for later use – it's so easy to dip each piece just before you will need to be using it.

One word of warning – be careful not to tread on the cane (the lengths of the cane make this very easy). The cane will split length-ways and a split, once started, has a nasty tendency to creep up the length. Discard split pieces – they will spoil the appearance of the chair. Prepare the cane as you need it.

Step 1 The first setting. Starting at the back, on the left, insert one end of the cane (if weaving with two sizes, use the thinner one) into the hole next to the back left corner hole. Allow 10cm (4in) to protrude underneath the frame and place the cane so that the glossy surface is facing up when the cane is placed across the frame. Peg the cane in the hole so that the cane is held firmly (fig.1).

Take the long end of the cane down through the hole at the front next to the corner hole. Make sure that the glossy side of the cane remains up and that there are no twists in the cane. Also make sure that the cane is not twisted as it goes through the hole. Pull the cane fairly tightly and peg it. Look at fig.2 for a detail of the complete pattern and the steps involved.

The cane is now brought up through the next hole, untwisted,

Below left: Peg the end to start the first step.
Below: Detail of the seven-step pattern.

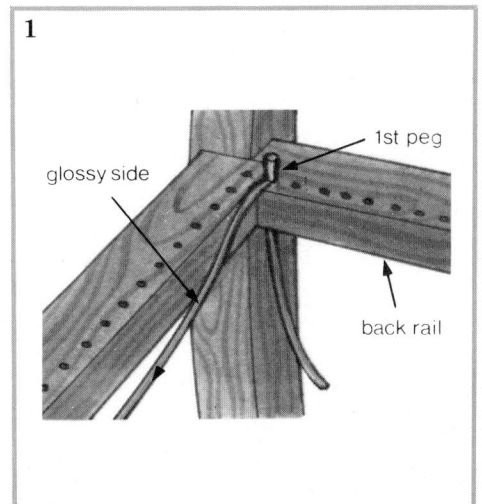

Step 1
Step 2
Step 3
Step 4
Step 5
Step 6
Step 7

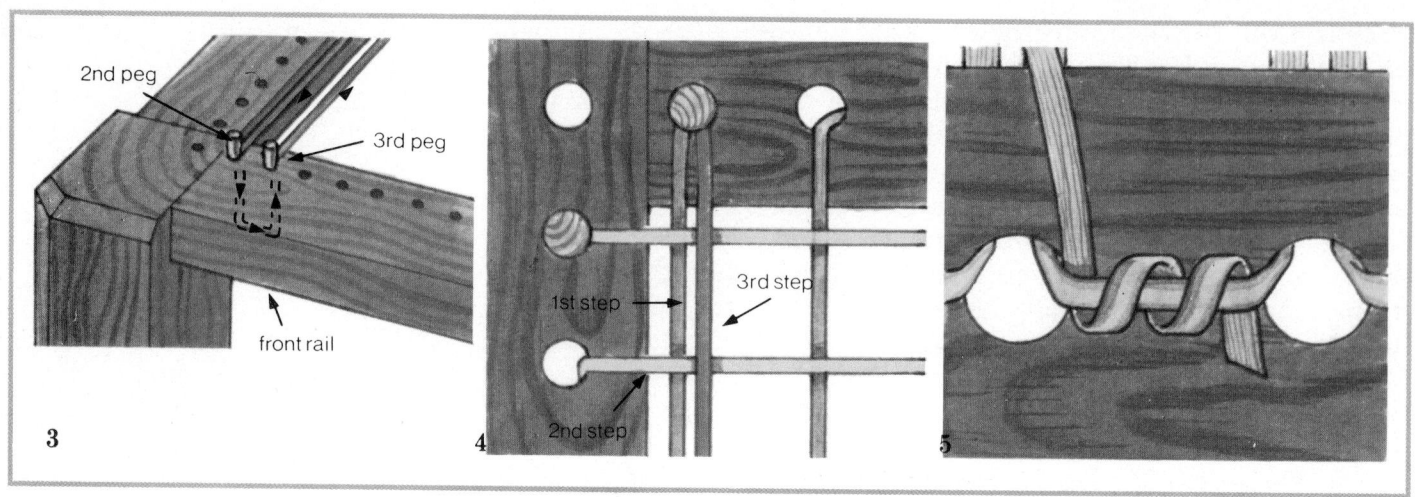

3 **4** **5**

3. Cane temporarily pegged.
4. The third step is parallel to the first step.
5. Tying in on the underside of the chair.

glossy side always facing – even on the underside of the frame. Pull tight and secure with another peg (fig.3). The cane is now passed to the opposite side to the hole next to the starting one. Take the third peg (or remove second peg) and use it to peg this hole.

The first peg is holding the cane end but each successive peg is taken from a hole to 'travel' with the weaving. Continue going backwards and forwards until the end is reached.

If the cane runs out, leave the end protruding from the underside and leave a peg in the hole to hold the cane securely until the ends are finished off. Then start a new length of cane in the next hole just as you started the first cane. Always leave 10cm (4in) protruding from the underside, for old and new lengths of cane.

Keep the tension fairly tight and even. Do not make it too tight – each successive stage tightens the work – but do not make it too loose either; the work must never sag of its own accord.

Step 2 is worked exactly the same as the first stage but going over the first step at complete right angles.

Step 3 The second setting. The first step is repeated on top of the previous two steps. The next step will be made easier by positioning the cane in this step so that it does not lie directly on top of the first step but is parallel to it – keep to the right of the first step, especially at the holes (fig.4). Try to plan the work so that you use the spaces on the underside of the frame that were not covered the first time. In other words, don't overlap the canes.

Tying in the ends see also Finishing ends. You can tie in the ends, if you wish, as you work. Pass the new end untwisted twice over the short strands on underside between holes (fig.5).

Step 4 is a repetition of Step 2 but, unlike Step 2, the cane must be woven under then over the vertical pieces (not over and under).

This step takes longer than any of the other steps. Run your fingers along a length of cane in both directions, and then use the cane so that it will be woven in the direction which feels smoother. Start as in Step 2 and peg one end. The cane must now be kept untwisted and the right way up. Starting from the fixed end, run the cane through your fingers, keeping it untwisted all the way to the working end. This is very important as there is no way of untwisting it once it is woven unless you unpick it. Having untwisted the cane, thread the end underneath the cane of the first setting (the one on the left) up between the two vertical canes and over the second setting.

Repeat with each pair of canes as you reach them. Do not pull the whole length of cane through until you have passed six pairs. As you pull the cane through it will flatten, straighten and tighten the work. Continue, backwards and forwards, joining in as required and pegging protruding ends.

Keep the pattern correct – remember that in this step the weaver always goes under the first setting and over the second. Don't worry too much about making the lines neat and tidy with close little squares – the next two steps will do this.

Step 5 The first diagonal. If you have been using thin cane now is the time to change to the next size (otherwise continue with No.4). Peg the cane end in the back left-hand corner. Start weaving over the first pair (horizontals), move over to the right by going under the vertical pair then over the next horizontal pair etc. The weaving appears to be done in 'steps' but once it is pulled through tightly it forms a diagonal line (see fig.2). If the chair frame is square you will end in the opposite corner, otherwise thread it into whichever hole that has been reached.

Bring the untwisted cane up through the next hole in front to the left and weave back. Keep the pattern correct – *over* horizontals and *under* the verticals. Weave like this until you finish off in the corner by passing straight across from one hole to the other.

Go back to the starting hole and start another cane (the corner holes are used twice) to fill the remainder of first diagonals. Go under the verticals, over horizontals, as before. Complete this weaving then check and make sure that the pattern is correct. Remember the only way to correct errors is to unpick the weaving. The weaving is usually easy, not needing tugging and pulling – if you find that you are having trouble check again that the pattern is correct. Then you can start the second diagonal.

Step 6 The second diagonal. This is exactly the opposite to Step 5. Start in another corner and weave at right angles to the previous diagonals. Corner holes are used twice again. This time the weavers

Above: The first four steps of the pattern are shown in sequence from the top to the bottom of the page.

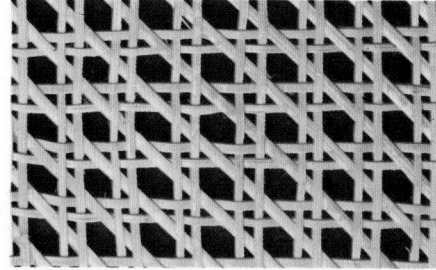

Above: The last three steps in the pattern are shown from top to bottom. The last and seventh step is the detail of beading.

Below: How to couch the beading into position.

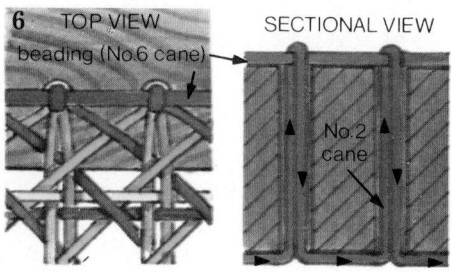

go *under* the horizontals and *over* the verticals.

Finishing ends By now the frame will have quite a lot of pegs holding various lengths of cane. These can now be tied if you have not done so already in preparation.

Dampen the ends to make them pliable. Cut each end to a point. Thread the end twice under a loop that is lying adjacent to it – use the bodkin if necessary to gently ease the cane into position. Keep the ends untwisted, glossy side outwards. Tap the 'coil' gently with a hammer to flatten it and cut the end off close.

If you have three or four ends coming out of the same hole, tying in can be awkward. Pass the cane to be tied under an adjacent loop then take it back under itself and cut off the end.

Pegs are used in blind corners and in holes which hold loose ends which cannot be tied in position. The pegs must fit tightly and once tapped in position they must be flush with the chair frame. If you are going to cover the frame holes with a cane beading, don't do this pegging until the beading is in position.

Step 7 Beading, a length of cane positioned around the outline of the weaving, is a fairly modern addition to the craft and is an optional extra. It can be put on with two different-sized canes, usually No. 2 and No.6 although there is no set rule and No.4 can be used if you prefer it for some reason.

The thicker cane is laid over the top of the holes and so hides them. The thick cane is couched down with the thinner cane. Beading is combined with either pegging or tying in. Tie in before starting the beading. Instructions are given as follows:

Start the beading by inserting a length of No. 2 cane into a hole next to a corner. Allow the end to protrude 4cm (1½in) towards the top. Bend this end down into the next hole and bring the long end up through the same hole. This method will secure the short end. Insert a length of No.6 cane down into the same hole and position it so that it lies over the holes along the side of the chair frame.

Pass the thinner cane over the thick cane and take it down the same hole. Pass this thin cane to the next hole on the underside – always untwisted, glossy side facing – and up through that hole. Take it over the thick cane and then down the same hole (fig.6). Continue to the corner hole and insert the thick and the thin cane into this hole. Start the two canes for the beading along the adjacent side before pegging the ends finally. Repeat this all around to complete the beading. Now complete the finishing touches.

Finally trim all the ends underneath. Make sure that all ends are tied or pegged before doing this. If the holes are very close together you will find it easier to do the beading with No.4 cane, otherwise couch the thick cane down through alternate holes instead.

Rush

Beginning rush work

Round mat

You will need :
12 thick rushes 12mm ($\frac{1}{2}$in)
diameter 41cm (16in) long. Cut
them from the butt (thick end) of
good quality rushes.
12-16 rushes for weaving.
Rush threader.

Rush baskets and matting have been made for centuries. The ancient Egyptians used rushes a great deal and even made rush boats on which to live. In England, during Tudor times, rushes were used to make a tallow light by dipping them into wax. Rush was also used as a floor covering for those who could afford it. Only a wealthy family could have the rushes changed more than once a year. Later on rushes were braided and sewn into mats which were longer lasting and formed a fabric effect.

Rush work is quite easy, even if you have never done any before. The colour and texture of natural rushes make them a joy to handle. Nowadays many beautiful articles are made, both useful and decorative, that blend with perfect harmony to our modern way of living. Rushes grow in still waters and slow moving rivers. Once harvested they are left to dry slowly. They are then tied into bolts and sold as such. The lengths of the rushes in a bolt vary – the average length is about 183cm (6ft).

Storage

Rushes should be stored in a dry airy place, preferably in the dark, so that the colour does not fade. A loft is a good place because a layer of dust helps to protect them. You can gather plants from the garden which are suitable for rush work. Irises, gladioli and montbretia, and many grasses, dry into rich golden brown colours and many of the tall plants from ponds are also suitable. Cut the plants towards the end of summer and leave them to dry. Then prepare them in the same way as rushes when you are ready to use them to make up into mats or baskets.

Preparation

Be careful how you handle the rushes while they are dry because they are very brittle and damage easily. Rushes must be wetted for about five minutes, either by sprinkling with a hose or watering-can in the garden, or by dipping the rushes in a bath of cold water. If you can put them out in the rain even better. The rushes are then wrapped up in a wet blanket, flannelette sheet or similar for a

Below: A rush threader or football lacing awl is used the thread the ends in the work.

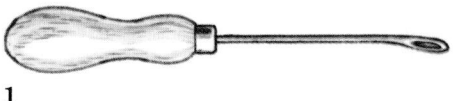

1

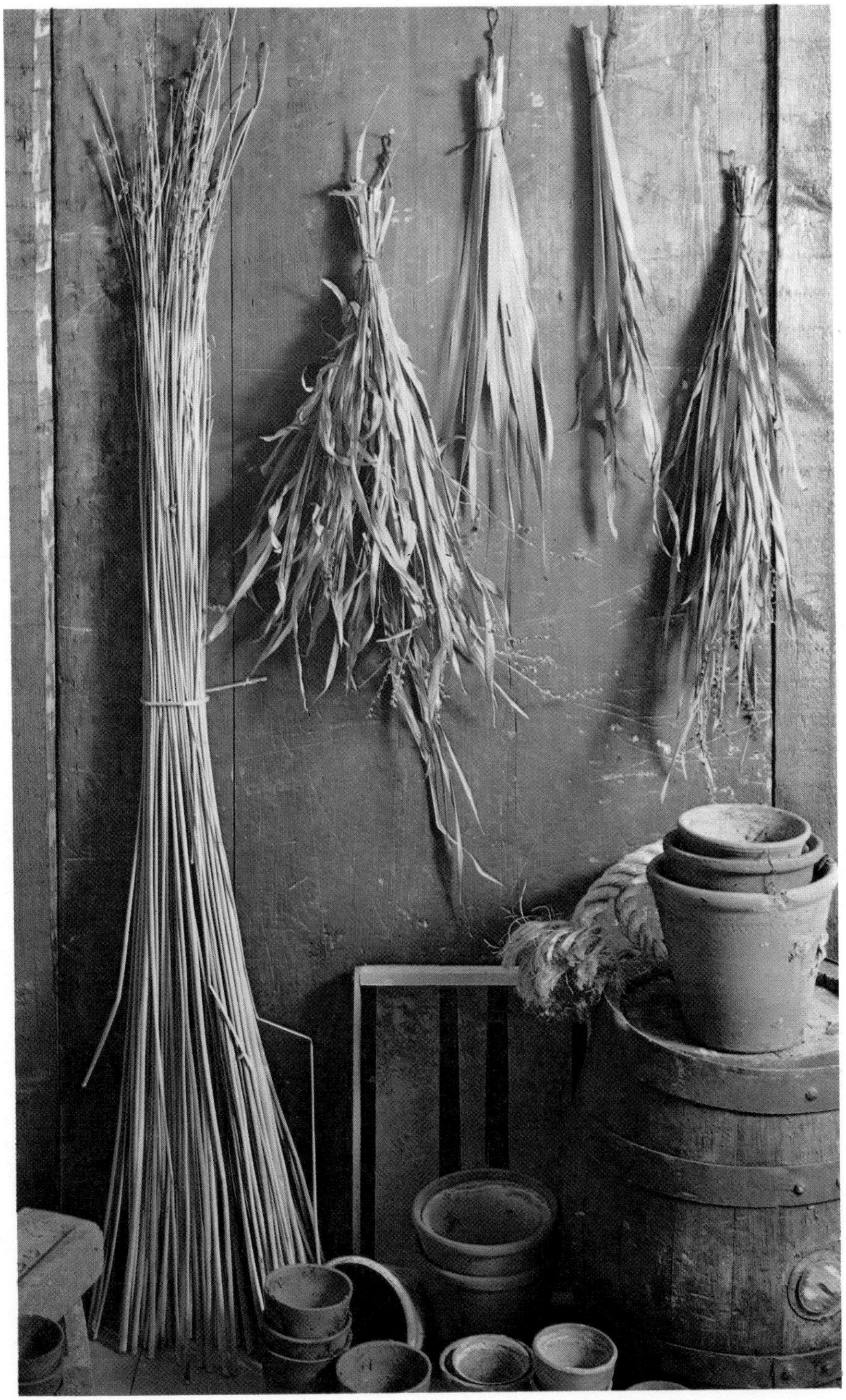

Left: Some of the grasses suitable for rush work include montbretia, gladioli, irises and rushes. Rushes are found in still and moving water. Once harvested they must dry slowly.

further three hours to mellow. It is a good idea to leave the rushes overnight so that they have all night to mellow and are ready for working in the following morning.

Before the rushes are used each rush must be prepared. The thin end must be tested for strength. Hold a rush in both hands about 15cm (6in) down from the brown flowery top (or thin end if it has lost its flower) and pull it apart with a gentle tug. Do not be too strong – just a little tug. Discard the broken end and try again another 15cm (6in) down until the rush is quite firm and does not snap. It is much less frustrating to get rid of the weak bits first, and so preventing the rushes from snapping when the weavers are pulled into place. You will soon get to know how much strength to use. If a rush snaps when weaving you will know you did not take enough away and if you chop it right up to the thick end, then you have been too heavy-handed.

Each rush must now be 'wiped'. This is partly to clean the rush and partly to remove all the air and water from inside the stem. Hold the stem in one hand at the thin end with a damp cloth in the other hand wipe along the rush, pressing it flat at the same time so that the water runs out of the thick end. If this is not done the work will shrink too much after weaving leaving it loose with gaps showing between the woven rushes.

Tools and equipment

The tools and equipment for rush work are very few and inexpensive. Apart from the blanket to wrap the rushes in and the damp cloth to wipe them, you will need a pair of scissors and a rush threader. A rush threader (fig.1) can be obtained from craft shops but a football lacing awl is just as good.

You will also need some form of frame or mould to build the baskets on – a block of wood, flower pots and biscuit tins all make good foundations for rush work. Later projects require string, or thread, both fine and coarse. Fine thread is used for sewing braids together and coarse thread for tying the work onto the mould. A large-eyed needle is required for the sewing.

The round mat

Start working by making a table mat to familiarize yourself with the tools and materials before starting baskets. The mat is about 20cm (8in) in diameter. When planning your own mats add 10cm (4in) extra to each end of each stake to allow for a border.

Right: A close-up photograph of three different kinds of flat rush work. Details are given for mats in the middle and far right.

Check weave Wipe the 12 thicker stakes to clean and flatten them. Lay six of them close together horizontally in front of you. Arrange the rushes with thick and thin ends alternating so that one side of the work does not finish more 'solid' than the other. Hold them on the table with your left hand to the left of the centre. Pick up, and hold in your left hand, the first (the one furthest away from you), third and fifth stakes.

Lay another stake across the second, fourth and sixth stakes close to your left hand as illustrated so that when the stakes in the left hand are returned to their starting position they form the first row of the check weave. Now the working order of the horizontal stakes will change and the second, fourth and sixth stakes will come up. You will achieve better results if you start picking up the next row while putting down the stakes you have just worked. For example, the order will be: no.2 up, no.1 down; no.4 up, no.3 down; no.6 up, no.5 down. Pull the stakes as they are put down to keep the check tight. Continue until all six vertical stakes are in place and your check weave centre is complete.

Pairing is done in the same way as when working with cane. Bend one of the weaving rushes not quite in the middle and loop it around the first stake on any side. Pair all the way around twice –

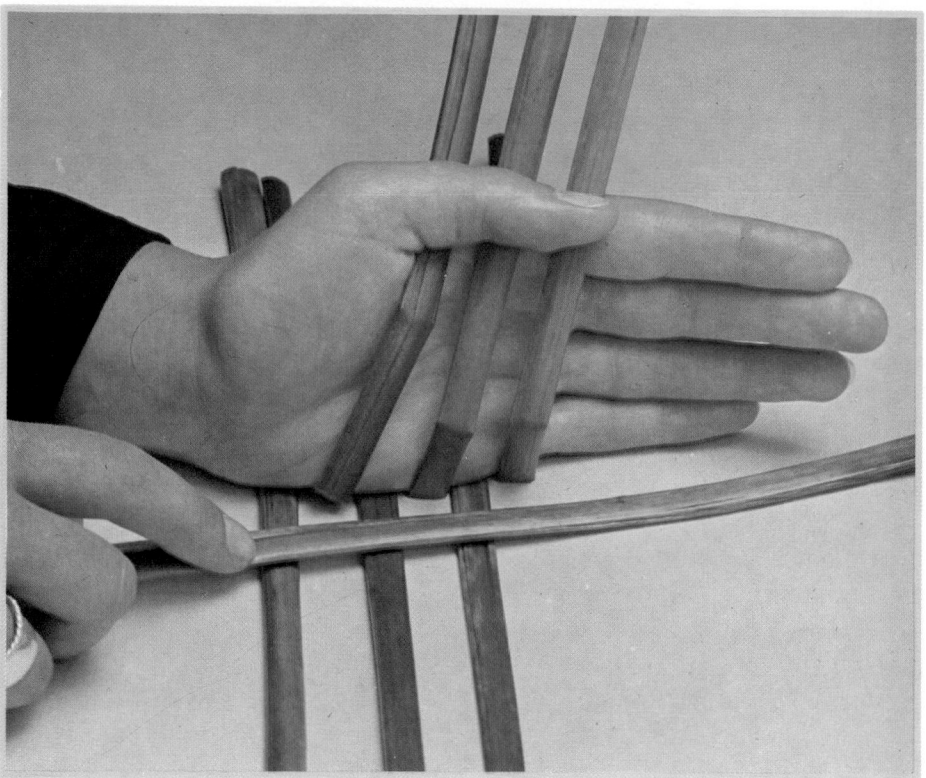

Right: The check weave is started with the left hand in position illustrated with the fingers holding alternate rushes to make room for the vertical stakes.

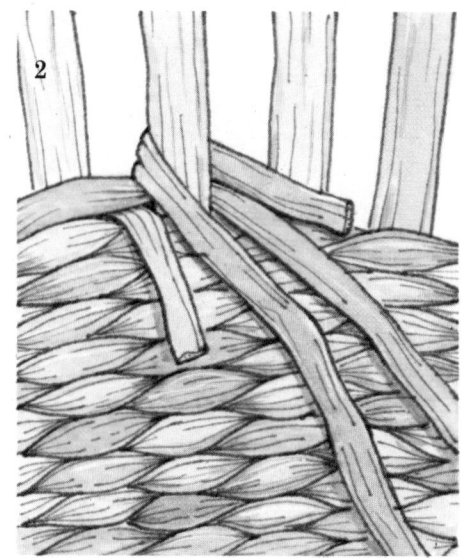
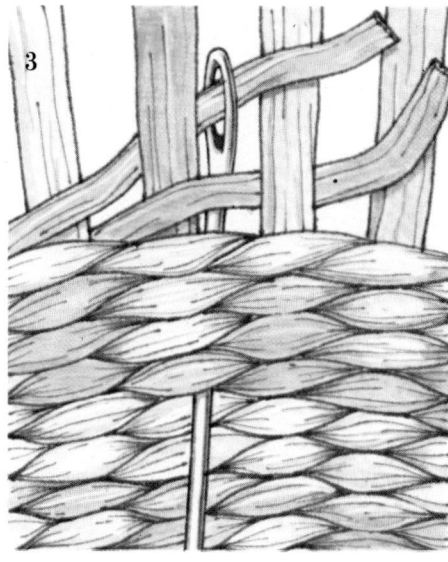

Far left: Joining in a new rush.
Left: Weaver end is threaded into the work.

left-hand weaver in front of one, behind the next and return to the front. Pull each rush down well at each pairing stroke.

Joining in a new rush. When a weaver has about 8cm (3in) left to weave and is in the position to be used next, loop the thin end of the new rush around the stake in between the two weavers. Loop it about 8cm (3in) from the end (fig.2).

Now both weavers have a long rush and a short end. Continue to pair weaving in the short ends as you go. If both ends run out together, loop the new one not quite in the middle and place it around the stake between the two short ends. Then once again you have two long ends. The two shorter ends are woven in together with the weaving as you go along.

Pair for two rounds, then make sure that all the stakes are central and that they are tight. Pull them into position if necessary. Spread the stakes out like the spokes of a wheel after the second round. Pair until the mat is 19cm ($7\frac{1}{2}$in) across.

The ends of both weavers are finished off by threading them into the weaving. Push the rush threader through the last four rounds of pairing, just where the pairing finished. Thread the weaver into the eye of the threader and pull it back through the pairing (fig.3). Repeat with the other weaver. A border is now added to complete the mat. Borders are described on page 93.

The oval mat

Oval mats are made in the same way as round mats but the stakes are cut into two different lengths. There are fat ovals and long slim ovals – you can make whichever you prefer. In basketry an oval is

Oval mat
You will need : 6 thick stakes 48cm (19in) long. 12 thick stakes 43cm (17in) long. 14-18 weaving rushes. Rush threader.

Right: Close-up detail of some of the simple borders that are suitable for edging rush mats. Make sure that the stakes are damp before you start.

merely an elongated circle. Some stakes will be longer than others. Allow for borders by adding an extra 10cm (4in) to each end of the stake. The mat measures 28cm by 23cm (11in by 9in).

Place the long stakes close together horizontally on the table. Place your left hand in the centre and lift up the 1st, 3rd and 5th stakes. Place the first short rush across remaining horizontal stakes. Continue to place five more of the short stakes into position to form a check weave at the centre of the mat.

Turn the work round and place the remaining short stakes into position. This will ensure that the block of check weave is in the centre of the stakes. Pair for 5cm (2in) then, if you wish start Border No.3. Continue to pair for a further five rounds and finish off. If you wish to have one of the first two borders, pair for 8cm (3in) before bordering down.

When you have completed the mat with its border, its appearance is improved if it is pressed flat. Place the mat between a newspaper and put some heavy books on top. Leave it overnight.

Borders

There are a number of simple borders that can be used in rush work and that are suitable for mats. Make sure the stakes are damp enough before you start working with them.

Border No.1 Push the threader up through the last four rounds of pairing as you did to finish off the weaving. Thread the stake from the next channel to the left into the threader and pull it back through the pairing. Try to turn the stake over to the right before it is finally pulled down. Do not let it twist in various ways. If they are all turned down in the same way the border will look even.

Continue all the way around then give each one an extra pull to tighten the work. When you are satisfied that all the stakes are all in place, cut each one off at the point where it emerges from the pairing. If you pull the stake just a fraction before cutting the end will spring up a little and will be hidden in the weaving.

Border No.2 This border is exactly the same as the first border but the stake from the second channel to the left is threaded through the threader and pulled into the weaving. Finish as before.

Border No.3 When you have about five more rounds of pairing to do, flatten each stake in turn and bend it right up and over itself a set distance from the weaving. Allow for the five rounds of pairing – 2.5cm (1in) – and the amount you want the stakes to protrude at the end. Devise some sort of gauge to make all the bends the same distance from the weaving. Pair around each stake as it is folded into position. Continue with the remaining rounds of pairing and cut off the ends of the stakes to finish.

Twist handles and borders

The instructions in this chapter include making a bowl which is partly chain paired and finished with a two-rod border. Prepare the rushes before starting work as previously described.

The flower basket

The basket is a flat round mat with a handle. Make the round mat exactly as before using the same materials. You will need two additional thick rushes for the handle. Before the mat dries out, bend up opposite edges and tie in position.

For the handle cut the two rushes about 1m (39in) long. Push both of them together through one of the raised sides of the basket under the third row of pairing. Use the threader to help you. Pull the rushes through until you have four equal lengths and bend them up to meet each other with the ends together.

Take hold of a thick end and a thin end in each hand. (This will help to keep the twist even all the way across.)

Try to anchor the basket somehow or get somebody to hold it for you. Now twist the two rushes in the right hand twice, then pass them over the left hand rushes. Change your hands over on the rushes. Repeat the twist and change-over until you have a sufficient length of handle for your purposes.

This method of making a twisted handle makes it firm and places the twists in the right places. If you just twist the rushes around together in one hand they will be loose and uneven.

Finish the handle by pushing one end from each twist into the weaving at the third round of pairing. Do this from the inside. Push the remaining two ends in the same place but from the outside to the inside. You should have two ends on the inside and two ends on the outside of the basket exactly opposite the starting point of the handle. Weave all the ends in and out of the pairing once or twice. Keep the basket tied into shape until it is completely dry. This prevents it from becoming distorted.

Alternative border

Another border can be used to vary designs.

Opposite: A delightful rustic basket shaped from a flat round mat. It can be made in a variety of sizes, with different borders and looks lovely filled with fruit, nuts or flowers.

Right: A handle is made from two rushes which are twisted together and then woven into the mat base.

Border No.4 This border is similar to border no.3 but each of the stakes must be turned twice before being paired. The first turn must be at the level you want the border to be. Turn the stake at right angles to itself and place it so that it is lying crossways – it does not matter which way you turn it (fig.1). Make the second turn so that the end is lying over the pairing and the two turns have formed a neat point (fig.2). Pair each one in as you go. This border is reversible as all the borders are but the appearance is quite different on each side. Either side may be used as the right side.

1. Turn the stake at right-angles to itself and place it lying crossways.
2. Make the second turn to form a neat point.
Below: A detail of the completed border.

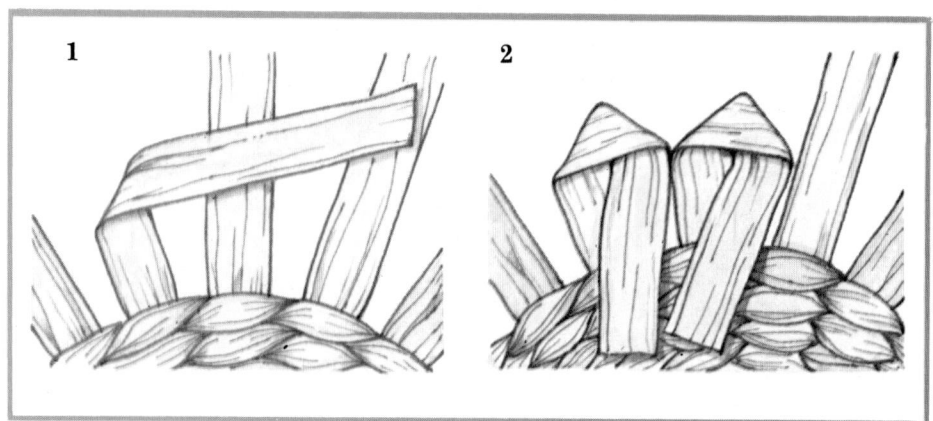

The large bowl

The bowl has a diameter of 35cm (14in) and is suitable for fruit etc.
Start as before for the round mat with the check weave but this
time use all the stakes double, ie use two rushes to form one stake.
Put on 4cm (1½in) of pairing still keeping the stakes double.

Waling is done in the same way as for cane work but there is no
step-up. Add a third weaver to get started. Wale for three rounds.
Pair for one round opening all the stakes singly.

Chain pair for six more rounds. Wale for three rounds pulling the
weaving tight to draw up the edges.

Two-rod border You can work any of the simpler borders or try a
two-rod border. Hold the bowl with the underside towards you.
Bend down any stake (1), behind the next (2), then 2 behind 3 (fig.3).

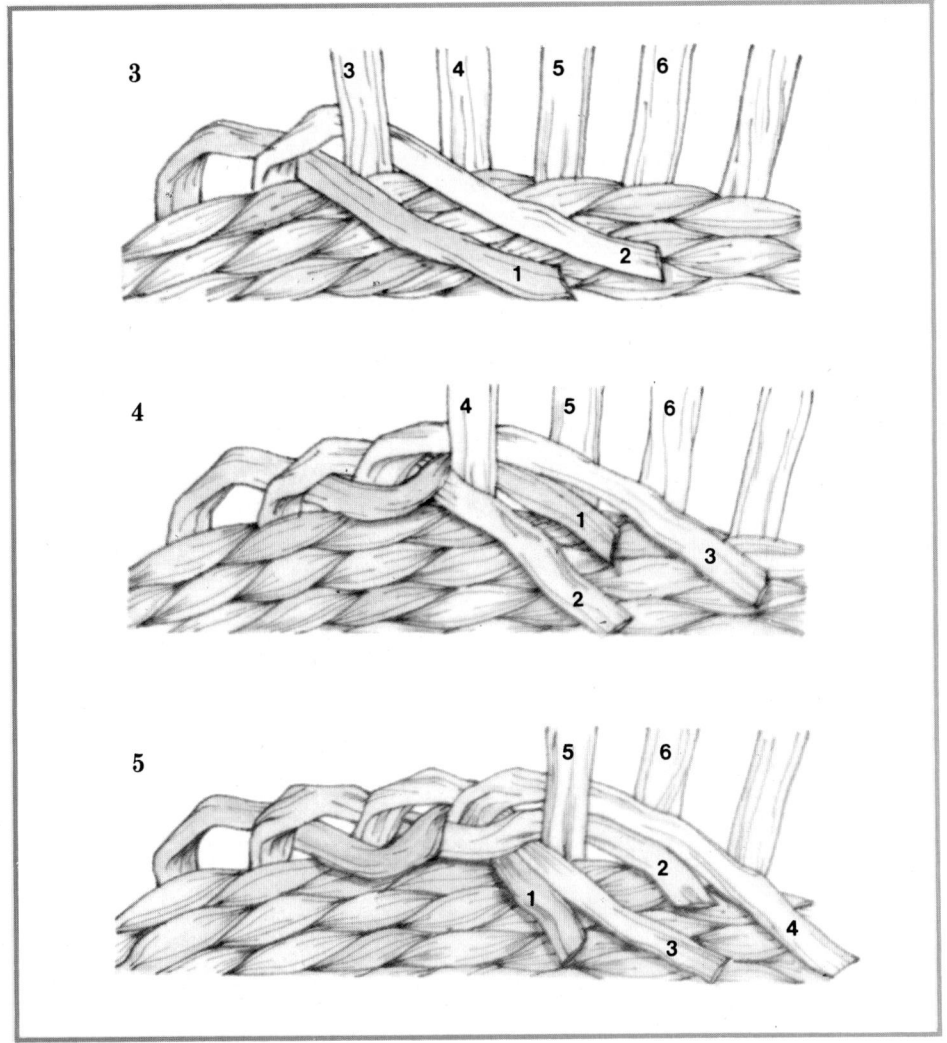

Large bowl
You will need : 32 thick rushes, 66cm (26in) long. 40-45 weaving rushes. Rush threader.

3. Starting the border.
4. Second stage of border.
5. Weavers form pairs.

97

Take stake 1 in front of stake 3, behind stake 4 and back to the front. Bend down stake 3 to lie beside but behind it (fig.4).

Take stake 2 in front of stake 4, behind stake 5 and back to the front. Bend down stake 4 to lie beside but behind it (fig.5). Take the longer of the left pair (the third stake from the right) in front of one and behind one and bend the next upright down behind it. In other words it is similar to a three-rod border but with two pairs instead of three as in the other type of border.

When you are left with one upright stake take the third from the right in front of the last upright stake and under the elbow of the first stake. Bend down the last stake under the first elbow. Weave the third from the right under the elbow of the second stake and the right-hand one of the last pair under the elbow of the third stake.

Neaten all the ends by pulling them tight so that the border pulls the bowl in a bit more, and then cut off about 6mm ($\frac{1}{4}$in) below the border. Do not cut them off too tight as they have a tendency to slip through when the bowl is in use.

Right: This magnificent rush bowl has been made with a two-rod border to finish the edges. It is ideal for use as a container for bread, cheese or fruit.
Below: A detail photograph showing a section of the same bowl as the one above, with the focus on the chain pairing which has been woven between the two sections of waling.

Upsett rush work

Rush baskets are no more difficult to make than the simplest mats. The basket illustrated incorporates most of the techniques that you have already learned, plus a new weave, border and a new way of upsetting. Unlike cane basketry which almost has set techniques for set places, rush work is much more flexible and any weave or any border is suitable according to your taste.

Moulds

You will need a mould of some sort. Any shape or size will do (as long as it is not too big) and whatever the shape and size of the mould is, your basket will finish the same. Some everyday articles make excellent moulds – large flower pots (the earthenware type is easiest to cope with as the rushes slip against the plastic ones) make lovely rush waste paper baskets or add a handle and you have a bucket bag. Toffee tins and larger fruit tins can be used to make small flower or needle work baskets and a larger, square shopping basket can be made on a large block of wood or two wooden seed boxes stapled together. Try to find a mould that is firm and strong and will not disintegrate when the wet rushes are put on it. If the ideal shape is a cardboard box pack it with books or blocks of wood to keep it quite firm throughout the work.

The stakes

Having decided on the mould, the next thing to do is to work out how many stakes to use and how long they should be.

To find the number of rushes measure around the mould, anywhere if it is straight sided, but about 8cm (3in) up from the base if it flows out. If the rushes are about 12mm ($\frac{1}{2}$in) wide allow one rush per 2.5cm (1in). Allow more if the rushes are thinner and less if they are thicker as a working average.

To find the length of the rushes for a round or square basket measure from the point where you want the border to be on one

Left: With proper care, this beautiful rush shopping basket will last for years. It is made with a diagonal weave.

side, down under and across the base and up the other side to the border again. Add to this measurement enough for two borders, one at each end of the rush; allow 10cm-15cm (4in-6in) at each end for a simple border and 15cm-20cm (6in-8in) for more intricate borders. If the mould is oval or oblong there will be two different measurements – one around the narrower part of the mould and the other around the wider part. Of course you will have to work out how many of each of these you will need by measuring across the short and long sides. If the mould is round or oval, and you have established how many and how long the rushes should be, start in exactly the same way as for the round or oval mats but use two rushes for each stake (without increasing the number calculated) to make them thicker. Open the stakes out singly on the third round of pairing. Pair until it fits the base of the mould then continue with the instructions below to tie the work onto the mould. In this way you will build up the shape.

Oblong shopping basket

The basket measures 32cm by 13cm (13in by 5in) and is 21cm ($8\frac{1}{4}$in) high excluding the handle.

The base Depending on the thickness of the rushes cut about ten stakes 117cm (46in) long for the narrow sides and about 26 stakes 96cm (38in) long for the wide sides – all from the stoutest rushes in the bundle. Check these before you use them.

Place the box (or mould) upside down on the table and put the ten long weavers over the base along its length, closely side by side, ready for the check weaving. See that they are centred. With adhesive tape, stick these stakes onto the box in the middle and at one end. Make sure that all the stakes are in order, flattened and securely held. Now you are ready to weave.

Start the check weave at the centre and work towards the untaped end. Continue to add in more short stakes until the edge of the base is reached. Stick this end in place on the mould and remove the adhesive tape from the centre and other end. Re-tape at the centre over the top of the check weave. Turn the base around and complete the other half of the check weave. Check that all the stakes are right and central and that all the stakes lie on top of the box and are not falling over the side and spoiling the shape.

The upsett You can either add a ridge, or turn all the stakes up the side of the mould and pair or wale. A firm ridge can be made quite easily for the basket to stand on. Tie the check weave base onto the mould with the string. Tie it up firmly like a parcel with the check weave on top. Put a ridge on before turning the work over.

Take each stake (1) in turn and bring it up and over the next stake

Oblong shopping basket

You will need :
About half a bolt of rushes – according to thickness of rushes.
3m (3yd) soft string to tie the basket to the mould.
A wooden block or similar mould. The mould used for the basket illustrated was a strong cardboard box (packed with books) and measuring 32cm by 13cm (13in by 5in), the perimeter therefore measures 90cm (36in).
Adhesive tape.
Rush threader.

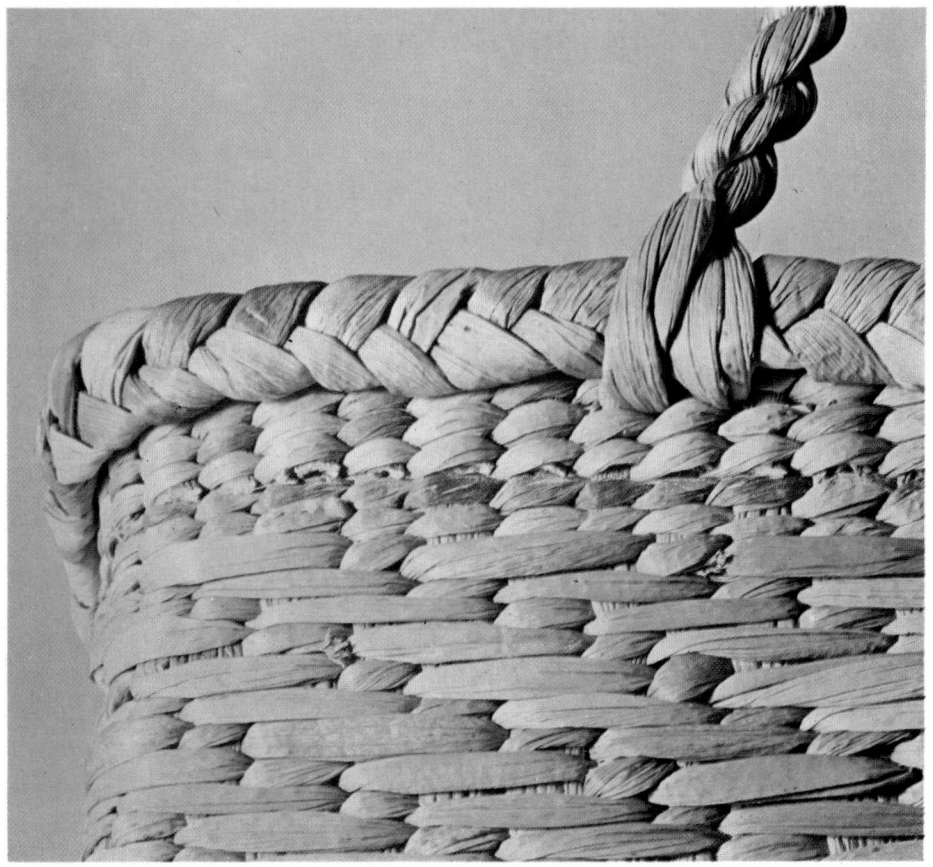

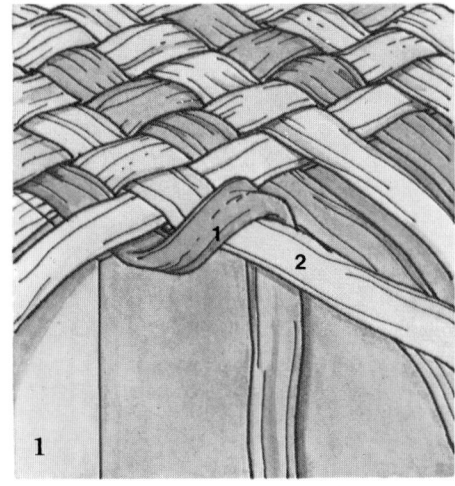

Above: Starting ridge for upsett.
Left: Detail of the basket
showing diagonal weave, pairing
and plait [braid] *border.*

(2) to the right. Hold stake 2 horizontally so that stake 1 has something to turn over, then lay this stake (1) in place against the side of the mould, so each stake is moving up one place (fig.1).

Repeat all the way around. The last stake of all will have to be threaded through the elbow of the first stake to complete the pattern. For an even ridge try to turn each stake in exactly the same way around its neighbour, rather than just pulling around anyhow. Pair for six rounds. Follow the shape of the mould closely, do not let the work come away from the mould. Watch the corners and make sure that the stakes next to the corners stay on the correct sides. It's very easy to let them slip round with the weaving and this will spoil the appearance of the basket.

A diagonal weave is a variation of pairing and the two weavers that you have been using for the pairing can be continued. For this weave the stakes must be in multiples of four plus one, or minus one. In other words it could be 35 or 37.

If the number of stakes is divisible by four plus one, then the diagonal weave will slant upwards from left to right and if it is

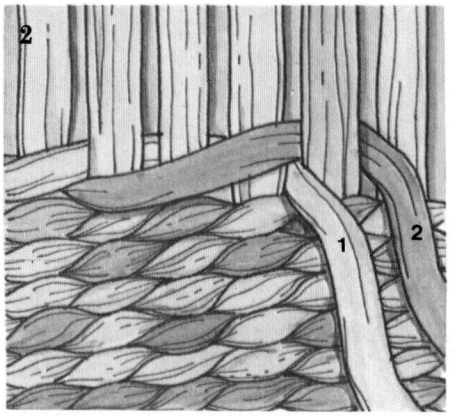
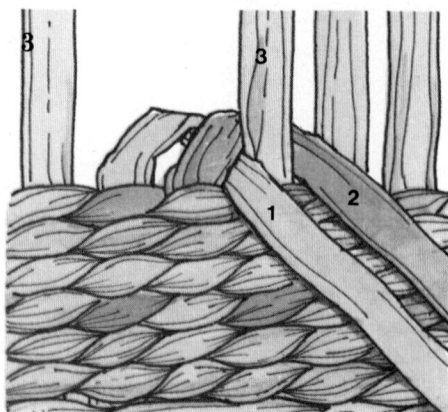

Far right: Starting the diagonal weave.
Right: The first stage of the plait [braid] border.

minus one then the diagonal weave will slant upwards from right to left. Choose which direction you prefer.

Remember that for this basket 36 rushes were cut which gives 72 side stakes (each rush making a stake on two opposite sides of the basket). As this number is divisible by four, one stake has to be dropped or added. As the stakes were rather close in this particular basket two stakes were woven together for a few rounds then the inner one was cut off.

To add a stake select a similar sized rush to match the other stakes, cut it about 31cm (16in) long and thread it with the threader into the pairing at a place where the stakes are least crowded.

Continue with the same weavers as for the pairing. Pass the left-hand weaver in front of one stake, behind three and back to the front. Now take the other weaver (now also the left-hand one) in front of three, behind one and back to the front (fig.2). Keep weaving around and around in this way. Check at the end of the first round that the pattern has come right. Once the pattern is established it is easy to keep checking.

To join in a new rush for diagonal weaving, you will find it easier to keep the rushes straight if you loop the new rush around a single stake. If you loop around the triple stake it tends to pull them in together. You will need to leave at least 8cm (3in) of the old weaver when joining to get a good tie-in for the short ends. Continue this weave for 15cm (6in). Revert to ordinary pairing for six rounds.

Plait [braid] border This chunky border is often called a plait [braid] or mock plait [braid] border, but its true name is a vale border. Before starting the border check the following:

Are the stakes still soft enough for a border or are they dry and crackly? If they are, re-wet them for a few moments and then re-flatten them to squeeze out the air and water to give them a good shape and to prevent distortion.

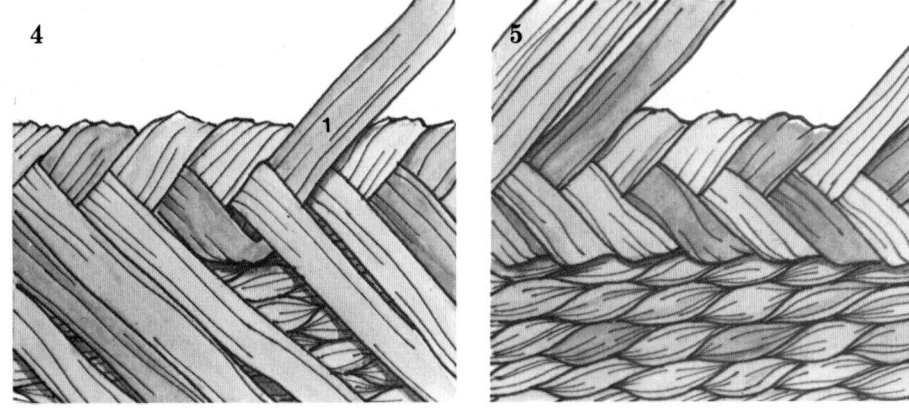

Far left: Second stage of the plait [braid] border.
Left: Finishing up the plait [braid] border.

Replace any broken or badly coloured stakes by threading a new one into the top pairing with the threader. Do not cut off the old one until the new one is in place. Pull the new one well down beyond the pairing so that 5cm (2in) protrudes – then there is no chance of it slipping out accidentally while the border is being put on. Cut this end off after the border is completed.

Check that all the ends of the stakes are long enough – you will need about 20cm (8in). If not replace them as before (or if too many are short choose a simpler border).

Make quite sure that the last round of pairing is level all the way around. If not pull it up or push it down to make it so.

This border is put on in three stages – each one is completed before the next one is started. Proceed as instructed below.

Stage 1 (fig.3). Starting anywhere you like bend stake 1 behind stake 2 and leave it lying to the front of the basket. Bend stake 2 behind stake 3 and back to the front. Continue by bending each stake in turn behind the next stake to the right and back to the front. The last stake will pass under the elbow of the first stake. Try to fold each stake in exactly the same way and keep them all flat to create uniformity. (In actual fact this first step is hidden at the end so do not worry too much if you have not achieved an even edge.)

Stage 2 (fig.4). Start anywhere again, not necessarily the same place as before, turn stake 1 up, at an angle of 90°, and underneath the next stake to the right. Once again continue all the way around, the last stake bending up underneath the first stake. Check that all the bends are level – if not pull them tighter or slacken them off.

Stage 3 (fig.5). This time each stake in turn is taken right over the top of the basket to the inside, and is threaded into the pairing one stake to the right. Push the threader up through the last four rows of pairing (at any place) from the front of the basket, but allow the end to come out inside the basket. Thread the stake one place to the

Left: Two more examples of rush work made on moulds. Opposite: A rush hat made with a spider base at the crown, and a trac border to finish.

left into the threader and pull it right down through the pairing to the front of the basket. Repeat all the way around. Check that they are all even. Cut off the ends close to the pairing to finish.

The handles are just the same as the flower basket in the previous chapter except four rushes about 125cm (50in) are required.

Thread two of the rushes through under the border and the fifth row of pairing between the 7th and 8th stakes from the left corner, and two between the 8th and 9th. Get someone to hold the basket firmly for you. Pull the rushes through so that there are eight equal ends. Hold four in each hand and put on a twisted handle. Thread four of the ends through from inside to the outside and four from outside to inside between the seventh and eighth and eighth and ninth stakes from the right corner. Weave the ends away. Repeat with the other handle in exactly the same way.

Remove the mould from the basket and trim the inside if necessary. Return the mould to the basket and leave to dry.

Making
rush hats

Rush hats are very attractive and can be decorated in a variety of ways. They are extremely light, are easy to make and are long-lasting. If you are unable to obtain rushes try using irises, montbretia or gladioli. Prepare the rushes before starting the hat. Choose a suitable mould for your purposes.

A rush hat

The hat is made from fine rushes. Its shape depends on the mould used and of course the trimmings are optional.

Spider base – the hat is started with a spider base. Take seven rushes about 1cm ($\frac{3}{8}$in) across and tie them together in the centre with thread. The length is unimportant as they can be replaced if necessary before making the brim. Spread out the rushes on a table with each rush folded in half to make seven pairs (fig.1).

Using a fine weaver, pair for three rounds. Keep pairing close to the centre. After the third round open all the rushes to singles and continue to pair for another 18mm ($\frac{3}{4}$in).

Take seven rushes about 52cm (20in) long and 12mm ($\frac{1}{2}$in) wide. Thread the thin end of each into the pairing next to every alternate stake. Pair for one round and on the next round open all the stakes to singles – you will now have 21 stakes. Pair for 18mm ($\frac{3}{4}$in) with fine rushes. Add another rush to every third stake as before so that you have 28 stakes. You will now use your mould.

Tie the work onto the mould as described in the previous chapter. The rest of the weaving must follow the shape of the mould until the brim is started and forms the crown shape.

Pair for another 18mm ($\frac{3}{4}$in). The base should now measure about 13cm (5in) across. Select 28 rushes of similar thickness and about 45cm (18in) long and thread each into the pairing against an existing stake. Put on one round of pairing and on the next row open out all the stakes to singles so that there are 56 stakes. Pair for one more round before adding the stakes.

To complete the hat you will need stakes of a reasonably even thickness and long enough to put on the trac border. Start adding new rushes if necessary as you weave the sides of the crown. To do this, select a rush for each stake that is shorter than the additional rushes added to the first seven pairs. Thread each rush into the work in the same channel as the rush needing replacement. However, do not worry about this until necessary but make sure it is done in plenty of time before starting the border.

The top of the crown is now completed and the side of the crown can be put on. Make sure that the stakes fit closely around the mould or the weaving will be loose and untidy. If you have too many stakes and they overlap, weave two together at even spaces

---

Rush hat

You will need :
450g (1lb) fine rushes – the quantity will vary according to size and shape.
Linen thread and rush threader.
Mould – a milliner's hat block or use a plastic bowl and pad it with paper if necessary to equal the size of the head at the position of the hat band.

Left: Starting a spider base.

around the mould. If you have too few add in stakes by threading them into the pairing and securing them carefully.

The weave on the side of the hat shown is a diagonal weave but you can use another weave if you prefer. Make the sides about 9cm (3½in). Put on three rows of pairing to make the band part of the hat firm before you start making the brim.

Now the hat turns outwards for the brim. Turn the work upside down and upsett. Wale or pair for four rows keeping the brim quite flat. If you find this difficult, remove the mould and stuff the work with crumpled paper to retain the shape. Then place it crown side up flat on the table and wale round – this will keep the brim flat.

Trac border – start with any stake and stroke it to flatten it. Measure 11.5cm (4½in) from the waling, and bend the stake neatly over to the right. Pass this stake over and under the next six stakes to the right and thread it into the weaving alongside the next stake. Repeat with each stake in turn, making sure that each one is carefully turned over at exactly the same distance from the weaving as the previous one. Weave the last few stakes over and under the stakes that have already been turned down – keep the pattern correct all the way through your work.

Trim off all the ends. Shape the brim with your fingers to the shape that suits you best and allow the hat to dry in this position. Complete the hat with trimming of your choice.

Rush braiding and seating

You can experiment a great deal in rush work, but plenty of practice is needed first with weaving and braiding rushes. Braided rush floor mats are suitable for most homes, especially country cottages. Braiding mats is not difficult once the handling of the rushes has been mastered and many lovely patterns can be made. Choose thick rushes for floor matting and fine rushes for table mats. Designs can then be adapted to make decorative coiled designs and similar techniques can be used for bowls and work baskets. Start with some braiding (even if you do not use it) to get the feel of stroking and twisting the rushes so that they become firm and solid. Prepare the rushes as described in the introductory chapter on rushwork and its basic techniques (page 86).

Rush plaiting

Take three rushes and tie them together somewhere in the middle, but not in half or the ends will all run out at the same time and make the joining of new rushes difficult. Fine strong string or linen thread is used to tie the rushes. Always leave the ends of the string long enough to allow for sewing later on.

Loop the rushes, at the point where they are tied together, around a hook or a nail in the wall. Bring the six ends together and divide them into three pairs so that each pair has a thick and a thin end. This will keep the thickness of the braid constant. Although the braiding looks just the same as braided hair, in rush work only the right hand is used for actually braiding; the left hand merely holds the material in a static position without moving.

Hold two of the pairs in the left hand. Using the right hand twist the other pair, two or three times to the right, stroking and pulling the rushes at the same time, so that the two rushes look like one and are quite firm as a weaving unit.

Place the right-hand pair over the top of the centre pair and hold under the left thumb. Pass the left-hand pair over the top of the twisted rushes. The original right-hand pair is now the left-hand pair, the left-hand pair is in the centre and the centre pair is now the right-hand pair. You work with this pair next.

This pair is now ready to be worked by the right hand. Continue twisting the right-hand rushes, as before, with the right hand and then placing the rushes in the left hand by taking them over the centre pair. The left-hand pair is then placed over it so that the centre pair is on the right. Keep the width of the braid even. A marker can be used by slipping a ring of the required size over the braid. If the braid gets thicker the ring will not slip down along the braid and if the braid gets thinner the ring will become too loose.

To join in a new rush wait until the end to be replaced is about

Opposite: Table mats made from lengths of plaited [braided] rush, which have been coiled and stitched together.

10cm (4in) long and in the centre of the braid. Lay the new rush against the old so that the top end of the new rush protrudes 8cm (3in). When it is their turn twist all three together working with the old and the new. Continue braiding until the short end of the old rush is lost in the braid. Generally, a thick end should be replaced by a thick end and a thin end by a thin end in order to keep the braid even. At all times aim to keep the combined thickness of the six rushes even to create a smooth surface.

After braiding a length cut off all the ends of the new rushes as close as possible to the braid as well as any old ends which may be showing. Short lengths of braiding are suitable for table mats but floor mats will require a much longer braid.

Round mats

For a small round table mat, about 20cm (8in) in diameter, braid for about 4.6m (5yd). Make the braid 12mm ($\frac{1}{2}$in) thick. Do not finish off the ends. Press the braid flat by either passing it through a wringer or by pressing overnight beneath newspaper weighted with books. It is then ready for stitching.

Stitching Thread the string at the beginning of the braid onto a needle. Make a tight coil with the flat part of the braid forming the thickness of the mat. Stitch in position (fig.1).

Do not worry if the braid is not long enough for your requirements; re-wet the ends of the braid and continue with the rope for as long as you wish. Many rushworkers make the mats by braiding a length and then stitching the braiding before continuing.

To join in a new thread tie the old and the new threads together with a reef knot and continue to sew, pulling the knot through the rushes until the old thread is used.

To finish off a braided mat, cut off the underneath rush from each pair and weave the remaining three rushes into the braid of the previous row. Stitch into place.

Oval mats

To make an oval mat about 25cm by 35cm (10in by 14in) braid for 11m (12yd). Begin the coil by doubling back the end and stitching into position. The piece doubled back should equal the difference between the width and the length required – in this case 10cm (4in). Continue to stitch the braid round this elongated coil which will form an oval shape for your mat.

Coils

The mats can be made more interesting by adding a series of coils. Make a length of braid and mark the centre. Coil and stitch from

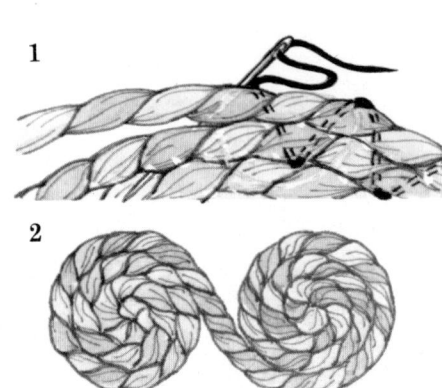

1. Stitching the plait [braid] to form a mat.
2. A double coil shape used for decoration.

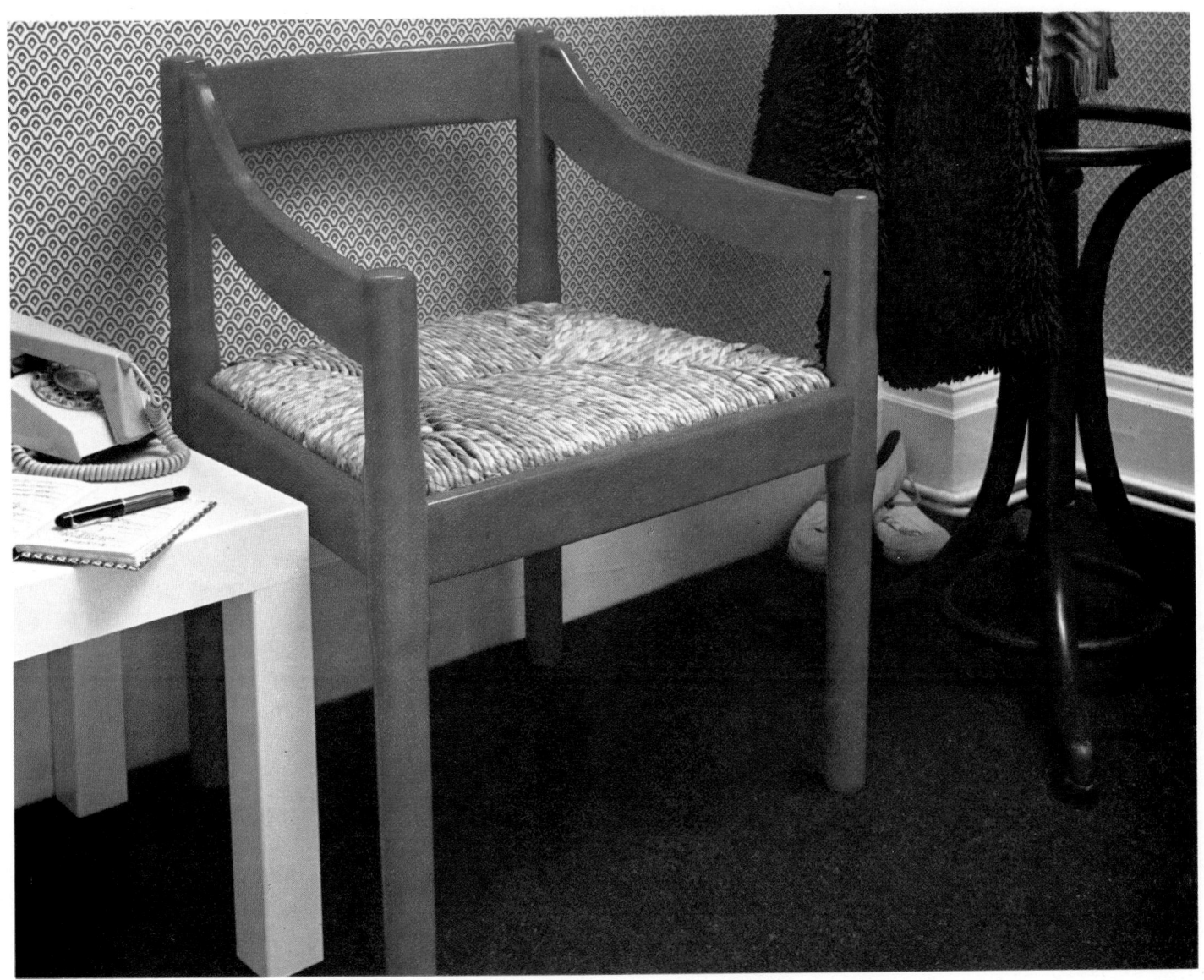

one end towards the centre. Stitch in the usual way. Bind the other end with the thread and then stitch towards the centre so that the two coils are opposite to each other (fig.2).

It is usual to have an odd number of coils so that the end of the last one is continued to form the braiding around the outside. In this way a sudden start is avoided and the sequence maintained.

Re-seating a chair

Rush seating is the ultimate in rush work. Often old rush seats need replacing – if you can repair them yourself it is well worth the

Above: A chair which has been seated with rush. This example is wider at the front than at the back.

effort. An average chair takes about three-quarters of a bolt to re-seat. No special equipment is necessary and, apart from rushes, the only other material required is string. Prepare the chair by stripping off all the old rushes and making sure that the joints of the wood are secure, especially in antique chairs.

A square chair or stool is started by tying two rushes – one thick end and one thin end – to a corner on the left-side rail, with string (fig.3). Make sure that they are tied very securely. Take the two rushes in the right hand and twist them to the right, stroking and pulling them quite firmly at the same time so that the two rushes look like one. Take the twisted rushes over and down the front rail at the corner (see fig.3). Now the rushes pass under the front rail and up through the chair untwisted. Twist the rushes to the left this time, stroke pull and twist, and then take them over the first twist, over and down the left-side rail. Pass under the left-side rail and all the way to the right-side rail untwisted.

Turn the chair around so that you can now repeat the looping process in this corner. Work each corner in this way (fig.4). The first twist in each corner is always to the right and the second one to the left. You may prefer to think of it as always twisting away from the corners. Try to use your right hand to do the right twist and your left hand to do the left twist. (So for once it does not matter whether you are left- or right-handed.) Keep the diagonal lines of the pattern at 45° from each corner and make sure each twisted pair is parallel to the side rails of the chair.

Join in a new rush by tying the old end and the new end together with a reef knot. Try to keep all the knots on the untwisted section between the rails where they will be covered and so hidden. At first this is easy but becomes increasingly difficult as the work progresses. Try to be patient however, and maintain this as much as possible.

3. Starting the rush seating.
4. Each corner of the seat is worked in turn.

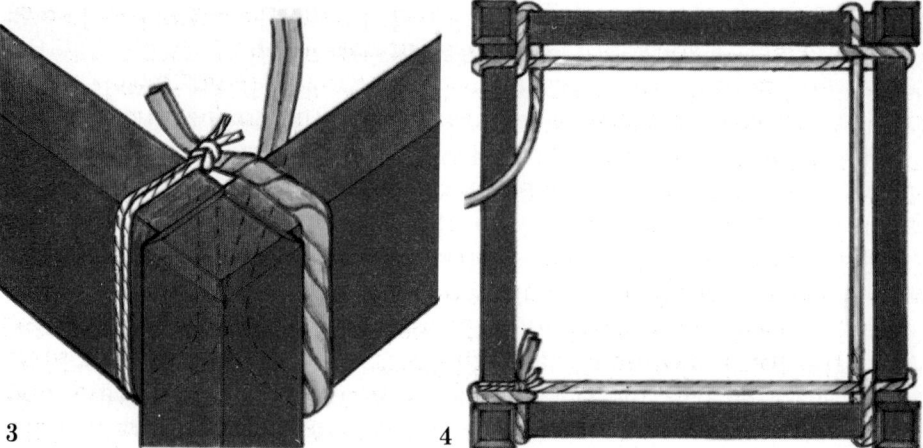

3

4

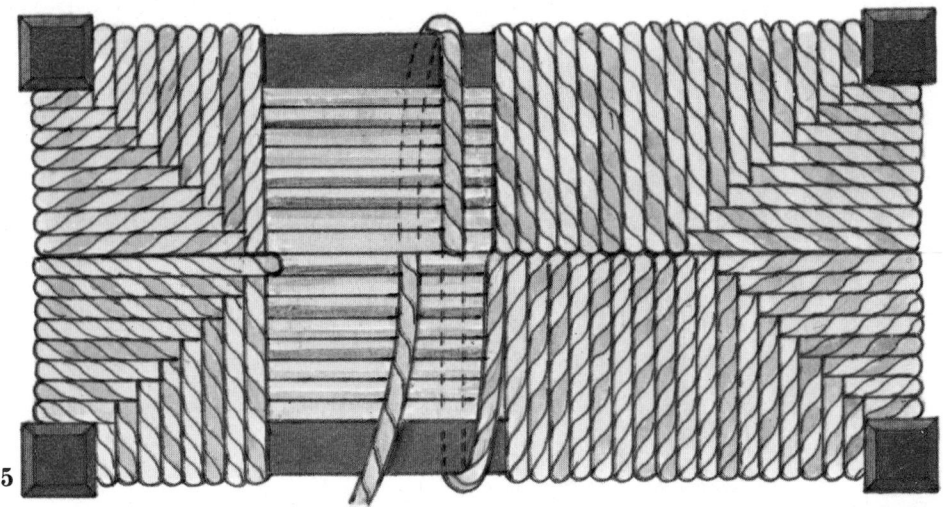

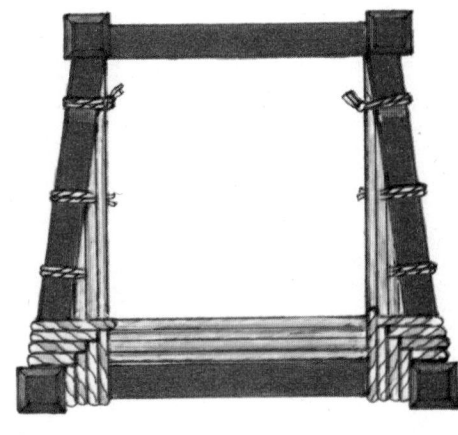

5

6

At the end the knots will show underneath the chair so keep them as neat as possible and turn the ends into the work.

Packing When you have finished about 12 rounds it is time to start 'packing' the chair. This is to make the rush work quite firm and even, and prevents the rails cutting the rushes. Turn the chair upside-down. Use any leftover oddments of dry rush for padding; the ends that have been trimmed, weak pieces, spotted rushes etc are all used up at this point. Cut them into short lengths and stuff them into the the eight pockets (two at each corner) formed by the pattern of the work. Push them right into the corners and make the padding quite firm and tight. Use a knife handle or something similar to help push the packing into the work.

Continue to rush the seat but do not attempt to do the whole chair in one session. The rushes should be allowed to dry and can be pushed up closer when starting to rush again. If you do it all at once the finished seat will be quite loose. Pad every dozen or so rounds and try to keep the rushes very tight. When the centre is reached tie the last rush onto the one opposite, underneath the chair.

Oblong shapes are started in the same way as a square chair. Work until the short side is filled up. Then continue to fill the long sides with a figure eight pattern between the two long sides (fig.5).

For a chair that has the front rail longer than the back rail (that is wider in the front) start as before (around the two front corners only), then tie the ends firmly against the right-hand rail. Now start all over again at the left side and weave only around the front two corners and tie off. Continue in this way until the area still to be rushed is exactly square (fig.6). Pad the corners if necessary. Then continue as before and work over the tie in pieces.

5. *Completing oblong shape.*
6. *Rushes are tied with string and worked around the frame to form a square shape.*

Straw

Introducing corn dollies

Corn dollies have been made for over 5000 years. They are found in various forms all over the world. They were generally made as fertility symbols. After the last sheaf of the harvest was cut it would be made into a corn dolly and great feasting and celebration would take place. Ceres, the goddess of the harvest, was thought to live in the corn dollies which were kept indoors during winter to protect the goddess. In the spring the corn dollies would be cast into the fields so that the goddess could help germinate the new corn.

Corn dollies were also used as sacrifices or in worship to a pagan god. Examples of corn dollies have been found in Mexico in the form of angels; Germany and Scandinavia also produced decorative objects made from corn and in Bulgaria they were made from maize. Corn dollies are not necessarily made in the form of 'dolls', but in a number of traditional, often symbolic shapes. The word doll or dolly is in fact a corruption of the word 'idol'.

In England different parts of the country made different types of corn dollies which have now become traditional. For example, a lantern is associated with Norfolk but a variation of it is also found in Hereford. A spiral is associated with Essex and fans are associated with Wales. These are just a few examples.

The braiding and weaving techniques used to make corn dollies can be used to make all sorts of decorative objects for the home. The corn dollies in themselves are decorative but they can be combined to make mobiles, or stars can be made for seasonal decorations. Children as well as grown-ups will enjoy making them.

The straw most commonly used to make corn dollies is wheat. The straw should have a hollow centre. Oats, rye and maize can also be used. Cut the wheat when it is nearly ripe as it will give a longer length with which to work. The wheat is cut just above the first join or node and usually below the ear to remove the sheath. Do not remove all the ears as they are used as well. Keep the wheat with the more attractive ears whole and try to select them in similar sizes. Fertilizer tends to make the wheat brittle so try to find wheat which has been grown with a minimum amount of fertilizer. Cutting the wheat can be a problem as the modern combine harvester threshes

Left: All sorts of objects are made by using the techniques for making corn dollies. This is a straw scythe.

and generally mangles the wheat, separating the grain, which makes it unsuitable. Cutting by hand is best but it can be tiresome if you want a great deal. A tractor driven binder will provide suitable wheat as it cuts cleanly and ties the sheaves without too much damage to the ears, or the straw itself.

Dry the straw by spreading it out on racks in the sun, but if this is not possible, bundles can be hung from rafters in a dry place or placed in an airing cupboard or in a slow oven with the door open. Once dry, straw can be stored for years.

Grade the straw before you work with it. Sort it out into two or three groups so that you have small, medium and large sizes. Compare the thickness of the wheat where it has been cut and the length of the stems and arrange them accordingly. Storage must be in a dry atmosphere to prevent the straw from going mouldy. Other hazards are mice, rats and seed eating birds like sparrows – they can do a lot of damage in a very short space of time.

Damping Once the straw has been dried it will split if it is braided. To prevent this the straw must be soaked in water. The time taken to soften the wheat varies – depending on how dry it is. Test the wheat by pinching it, if it does not split it is ready to use. Do not oversoak the wheat as it becomes too soft to handle with ease. Warm water will speed up the damping process. Do not let the ears get wet. Arrange a damp towel around the wheat while you are working – this prevents it from drying before you use it.

Corn dollies are often decorated with ribbons whose colours have different symbolic meanings. This Welsh fan is trimmed with red ribbon, symbolizing warmth.

120

Working with paper straw

Getting hold of straw is not always easy as it is seasonal but if you stock up on it you will have plenty to keep you busy. If you find it difficult to get straw or if you want to practise the techniques involved in making corn dollies, you can always use paper straws. These are more readily available from craft shops than are wheat straws. Paper straws have added advantages in that they can be glued or threaded together and they can be painted or dyed, thus making it possible to produce a wide variety of colourful decorations. They also look extremely effective.

Drinking straws can also be used but because they are waxed they cannot be coloured or glued. Paper straws are available in two sizes; the standard size is similar to a drinking straw, while the other size is slightly larger. All are suitable for this work.

Several types of colour can be used for decorating paper straws.

Powder or poster colours are best applied to the finished object as the dry paint rubs off during the handling.

Aerosol paints though more expensive, give a good all-over colour and help to make the finished model firmer. They also dry quickly.

Cold water dyes are an economical way to colour both finished objects and individual straws, but dip quickly to prevent the water softening the paper, then drain on newspaper. Handle wet objects with care to prevent them losing their shape. Use dyes according to the manufacturer's instructions but with half the recommended quantity of water. Test dip straws in the dye before embarking on a project to make sure you have the right colour.

Wood stains can also be used. Colours are not limited to shades generally associated with timber. In powder form the stains can be mixed with either water or methylated spirit. Again, test dye.

Inks can be used for bright, fast colours and also for colouring individual straws before working with them. Ink does not rub off in handling, so children can play quite safely.

Joining

Both wheat and paper straws are braided and woven the same way, but the joining methods are slightly different. Wheat tapers slightly

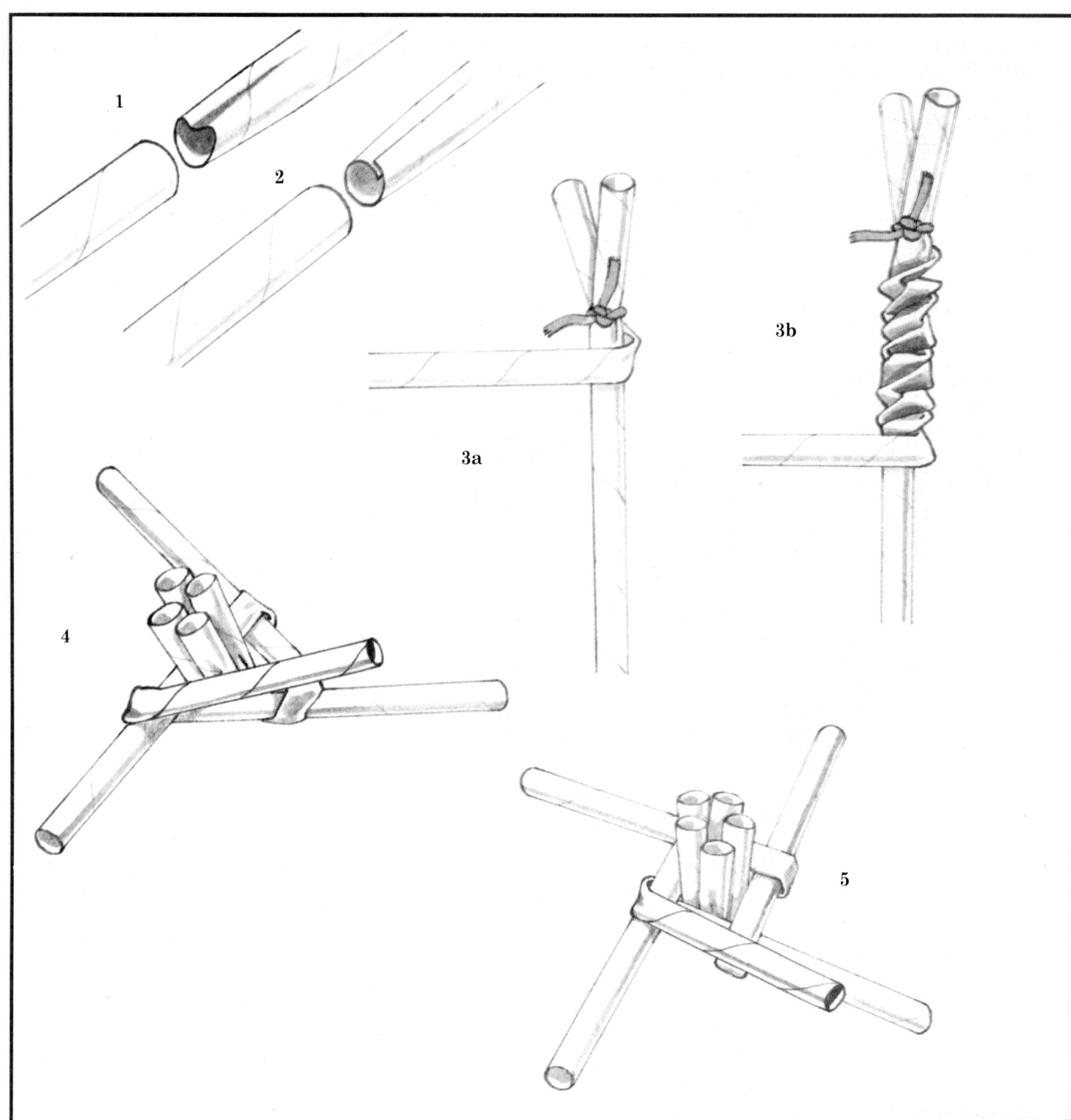

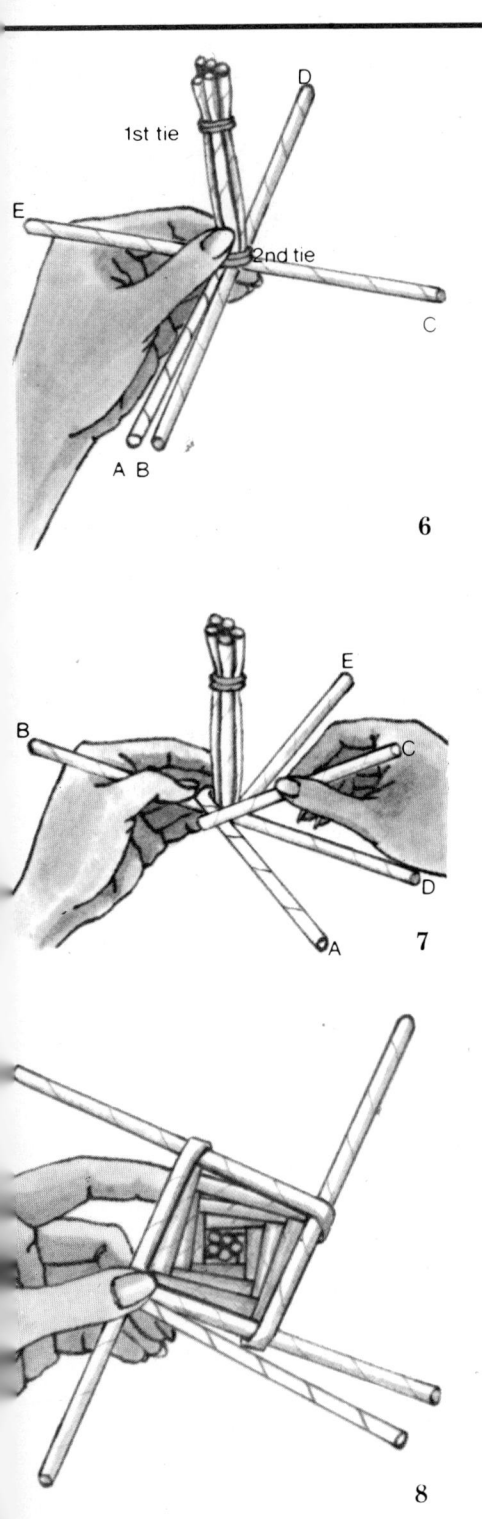

along its length, so the smaller end is pushed into the hollow larger end of another straw but paper straws all have the same diameter so cannot be joined like this.

To join paper straws run your fingernail lengthways along the end of the straw that is to fit inside the other straw and score it about 6mm ($\frac{1}{4}$in). Squeeze the end lightly so that the indentation makes a heart shape on the cross-section. Push this end into the other straw as far as it will go without denting or creasing either of the two straws (fig.1). This makes a strong join.

Another method is to cut a slit 18mm ($\frac{3}{4}$in) down the length of the straw, squeeze the straw lightly so that the cut edges overlap, then push this end into the end of another straw (fig.2). Wheat straws of the same diameter are also joined together like this. Try to join straws at a place where they will not have to be folded as it is difficult to bend a double thickness of straw. Bulky folds spoil the regularity of the weave and look unattractive.

Weaving

You can weave with any number of straws from four upwards. Two and three straws cannot be woven but can be twisted to make braids which were traditionally known as 'favours' and worn in the buttonhole. Braiding is simply the twisting together of straws of the same thickness. Instructions are given below.

To make a two-straw braid tie two straws firmly together at the top, hold them in the left hand at the knot and fold the first straw over the second so that the two straws form a right angle. Make a quarter turn clockwise and fold the second straw over the first (fig.3). Continue like this until you have the length you want.

Using more than two straws The shape of the objects being woven depends greatly on the number of straws used. Four straws, for example, produce a triangle in cross-section (fig.4), while five straws make a square (fig.5). The more straws you weave with, the rounder the shape will become and the firmer the object will be.

The five-straw braid is the basic weaving process for both corn dollies and paper straws. Once this has been mastered, it is fairly easy to tackle any number of straws up to about ten or 12. Weaving

1, 2. *Two ways are shown of joining paper straws.*
3a, 3b. *Forming a two-straw braid.*
4. *Four straws form a triangle shape.*
5. *Five straws form a square shape.*
6. *Starting a five-straw weave.*
7. *Working around the former.*
8. *First step to increase the width.*

around a central core (former) is the easiest way to work because the former helps to shape the weaving as it grows. After this, you can progress to free weaving working without a former.

Five-straw weave Tie the five straws together tightly about 2.5cm (1in) from one end and again about half way along the length of the straws. The distance between ties makes the former. (When working a free weave, omit the second tie.) Hold the straws in your left hand with the fastened ends upwards, forming the core.

Fan out the straws below the second tie so that they make a square. Three corners have one straw each and the fourth corner has two (fig.6), which will be nearest to you. Bend the straw nearest you (A) and lay it anti-clockwise over the next two straws close to the central former. This is the first stage.

Move the work clockwise so that the last straw you went over (C) is nearest to you. Hold the work lightly, trying not to flatten the straws. Take straw C up and over straws A and D (fig.7), again holding it against the central former.

Continue like this always taking the last straw you passed over and moving it anti-clockwise over the next two straws to produce a spiral. Remember always to turn the work towards you in a clockwise direction each time you move a straw. The neatness of the work as it builds up around the former depends on the regular folds of the working straws and avoiding joins at folds.

Shaping is controlled by laying the straws in certain positions. To keep a straight shape, each straw must be placed exactly over the straws underneath. Try to get this shape correct.

To increase the width take the straw over the next two in the usual way but lay it slightly outside the straws underneath (fig.8). Pull the next straw back under the overlying one, take it over and position it alongside the next straw (fig.9).

To decrease the width lay the straw slightly inside the underneath (fig.10). Obviously, when working around a former, you cannot decrease width, so this applies only after increasing or in free weaving. Do not try to hurry the shaping process or it will spoil the finished result. Create the shape very gradually.

To finish off tuck the ends of the straw into the weave. Glue is used on paper straws only when making pictures or collages or assembling woven pieces to complete an object. Use a quick-drying, clear adhesive so that the straws can be held in place while they dry. Thread may also be used to keep the straws together and is especially useful when making mobiles.

Paper straw mice
These delightful little mice are made by free weaving without a

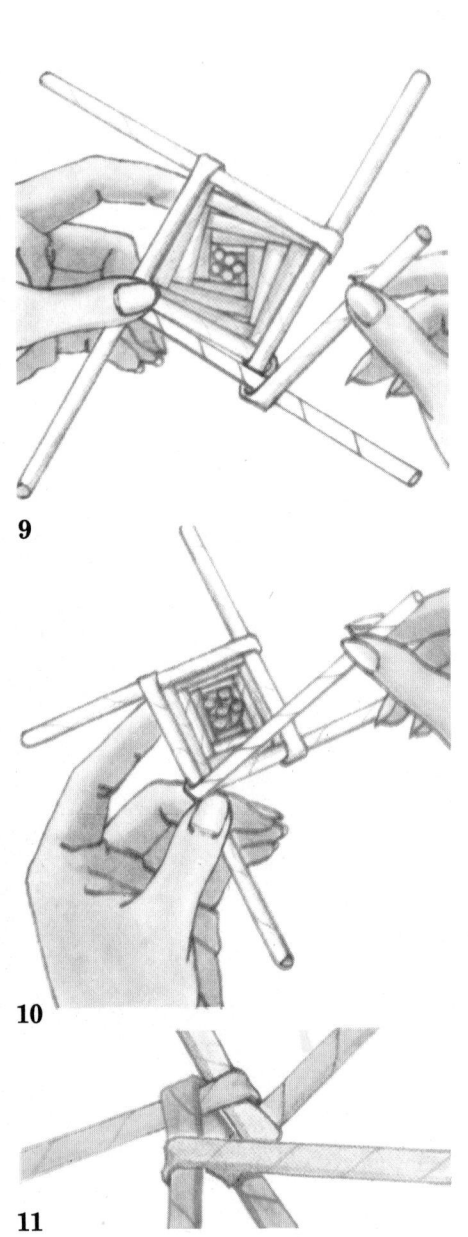

9

10

11

9. Second step to increase the width.
10. Decreasing the width.
11. Six-straw weave.

central former. The largest mouse is about 10cm (4in) long excluding the tail. Start a six-straw flat base weave without a former by taking three straws and placing them one on top of the other in a star shape (fig.11). Weave, but without a former, moving each straw over the next two. Increase as soon as you can to make the fat part of the mouse then gradually decrease, ending by tying the six straws together with white cotton and trimming to a point for the nose. For the tail, insert a flattened straw through the base weave. Use the two halves to make a two-straw braid. Glue the two ends together and cut to a point. Two pieces of flattened straws are stuck in place for the ears and another piece, fringed at both ends, is stuck in place for whiskers.

Below: These delightful mice are made from paper straws using the same technique for weaving corn dollies.

Traditional corn dollies

In the previous chapters you have learned how to cut, dry, store and dampen wheat straw and how to weave with paper straws. Having mastered these techniques, it is now possible to progress to making some of the traditional golden corn dollies that look so delightful hanging in a kitchen or serving as unusual table decorations. Another interesting use for them is to revive the old custom of making a baby rattle out of straw, enclosing inside either a small bell or a few beans to make an intriguing noise.

The materials for corn dolly making are simple enough: hollow-centred straw, such as wheat, oat, rye or maize; raffia, a sharp pair of scissors, wire and ribbon. The ribbons used to adorn traditional corn dollies have different meanings. Red stands for the poppy and for warmth, green for spring and fertility, blue for the cornflower and truth, yellow for the corn and the goddess Ceres, white for purity and brown for the earth. Remember to dampen the straw before working with it, to keep it flexible.

Five straw favour

These were often made by farm hands as love tokens for their sweethearts, and make delightful gifts.

Take five straws with the ears still in place and, with raffia, tie them together firmly just below the ears. Spread out the straws and work a five-straw weave without a former and with the ears dangling from the weave. Do not increase the size of the work, keep it constant along its entire length.

Leave a short length of unwoven straw at the end. Tie the straws where the weaving ends with raffia. Bend the braid into a loop and tie together above the ears. Trim off excess straw and decorate with a ribbon bow in a bright, attractive colour.

Suffolk horseshoe

The 'horseshoe' is another five-straw braid, like the 'favour' and the 'lantern'. You need a former to work around, and also 25 to 30 straws. For the former take about six 15cm (6in) long straws and a piece of wire the same length. Bind together.

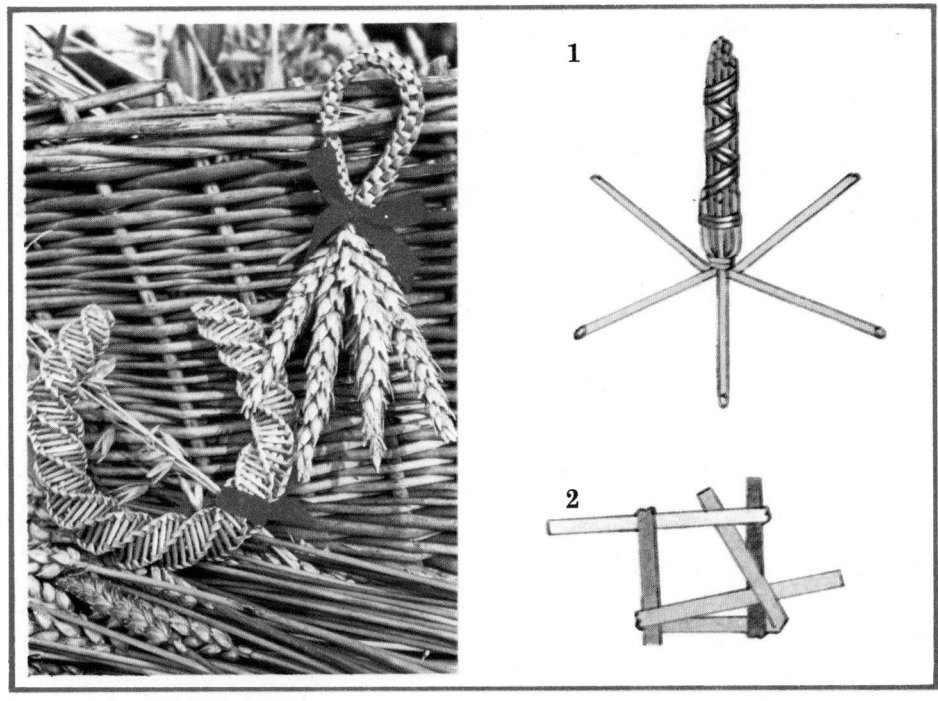

Far left: A horseshoe and a five-straw favour.
1. Working around former.
2. Straw is tucked under to finish.

Tie five straws onto the end of the former with the straws pointing away from the former and spread the straws into a five pointed star (fig.1). With the former pointed upwards, braid along the core using the decreasing braid all the time.

Close the end and finish off by tucking one straw under the opposite one (fig.2). Trim straw ends close to the braid and bend into a horseshoe-shape. Trim with a spray of oats (as a compliment to the horse) and a ribbon. If you have some experience doing the five-straw weave, you can bend the former into a horseshoe shape and then do the braiding afterwards.

The Herefordshire Lantern

Take five straws with the ears on them and about 30 without. Cut the ends at a slant to make joining easier. With raffia, tie five straws just below the ears. Work a five-straw weave and increase the size on every round. Join in new straws as required.

When the base of the lantern is the required size, start decreasing gradually, working until the work closes at the top. The spiral effect will appear as you decrease. When the work has closed, make sure that you have five long straws joined in. Continue braiding and make a loop to finish, or make four miniature lanterns and hang one from each corner. If you wish, you can use the lanterns to decorate your Christmas tree as an unusual touch.

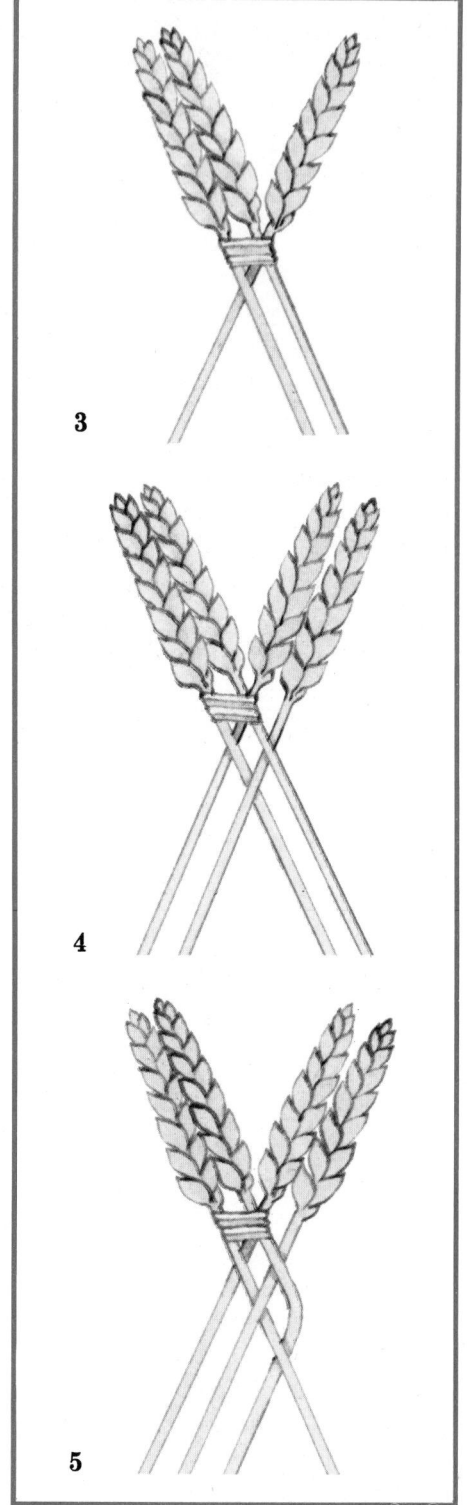

3

4

5

128

Short Welsh Fan

Prepare 29 long well-matched straws, each with the ears the same size and colour. Tie three firmly together just below the ears. Lay them flat on a table with the ears facing away from you (fig.3).

Ears of wheat have two sides to them, a rough and a smooth, so make sure the ears are all facing smooth side up. Keeping the smooth side of the ear uppermost, take a straw and put it under the outside one of the pair so that it lies parallel to the single one (fig.4). Lift up the inside one of the two straws on the right and lock it in place by folding the outside straw under it and across to the left, then replace the inside straw (fig.5). You now have one straw on the right and three on the left.

Insert another straw under the outside straw on the left-hand side (fig.6). Repeat the locking process (fig.7). Continue adding one straw on each side until you have a total of 13. As the ears may now begin to crowd together, do an extra locking weave on each side after adding each pair of straws, to secure them.

When all the straws have been used up, do five extra locking weaves alternately on each side. Bunch the straws together at the ends, tie with raffia and cut off the surplus straw. Keep flat while drying. To decorate, tie ribbons onto each bunch of straws. Choose the ribbon colour according to the meaning.

Opposite: Two traditional corn dolly lanterns from Yorkshire and Hereford.

3. Three straws are tied together to make the Welsh fan.
4. Fourth straw positioned parallel to single straw.
5. Right hand straw is folded under one and moved to left.
6. Straw added to lie parallel to single one.
7. The locking process is repeated on the left.

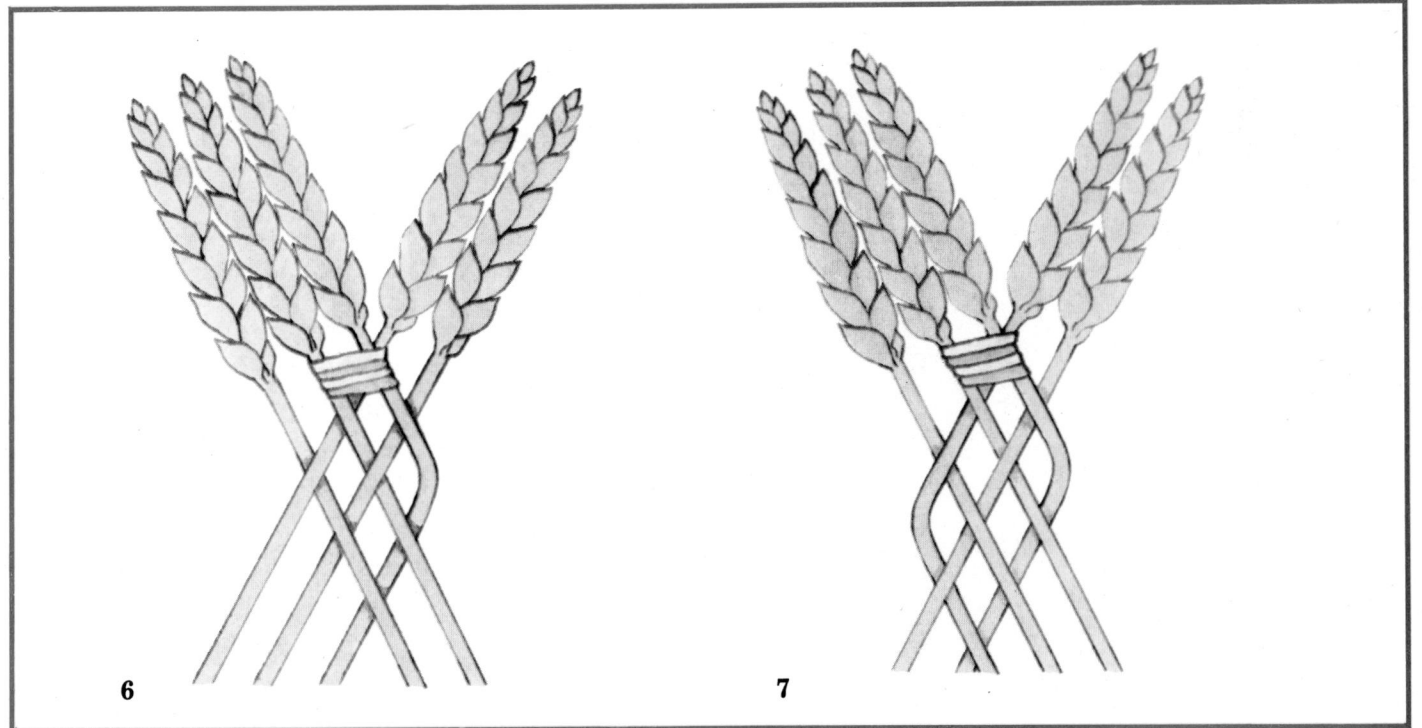

6   7

Making corn shuck dollies

Making dolls from corn husks is a craft originated by the American colonists who made them to decorate their homes and as toys. Early settlers called the corn husks 'shucks', and so the craft has become known in America as 'cornshuckery'.

Preparing and selecting

Selecting the corn needs some care. Try to choose ears with as much silk as possible. Buy the ear unopened and avoid tearing down the shuck to look at the golden kernels inside. Remove the shuck very carefully with a knife – cutting round the corn at the top and the bottom, then slowly unravelling the shucks one at a time without tearing them.

Save the silky strands inside the shuck, as they are used for dolls' hair. Each doll takes about five hours to make and two weeks to dry. You always work with wet shucks, which are blotted on a towel. If you are unable to complete the work in one sitting, the entire doll can be re-dampened and finished later. Corn dolls are made entirely by rolling and tying.

Shucks are the material from which the doll is made and, as in sewing, you will need large pieces of material for sleeves and skirts. If you carelessly remove the shucks, you will have only strips with which to work. The cut at the top of the shuck should be high enough to give a long length.

Drying and storing

When all the shucks have been cut, spread them individually in the sun to dry. Do not dry them in an oven, where even the lowest heat dries a shuck too quickly and makes it too brittle to use. On hot summer days, drying will take only a few days but in autumn it may take as long as a week. Make sure the shucks are completely dry before placing them in a polythene bag for later use or some may mildew. When you have enough, store the bags in a dry place.

If you gather shucks at seasonal intervals, you will find that early corn has blond corn silk, mid-season corn has silk suitable for red-headed dolls and late corn silk makes beautiful brunettes. A

bouffant hair-style will take the silk of about five ears of corn. Let the silk dry thoroughly in the sun for three to five days. Sort by colour and store in polythene bags separately from shucks.

Cornshuck dolls

Instructions are given for a man and a woman doll, 18cm (7in) high. You will be making two dolls at the same time, up to the moment when the woman receives a skirt and the man legs and a coat. Soak 20 of the whitest shucks in the plastic dish and work on the

These delightful dolls made from corn husks are a fine example of the American craft of cornshuckery.

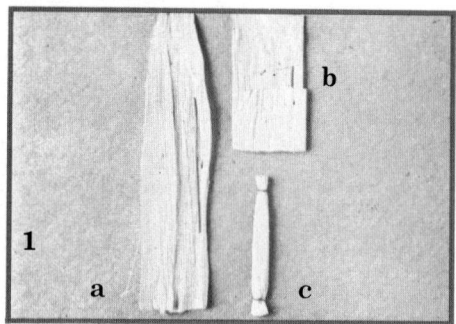

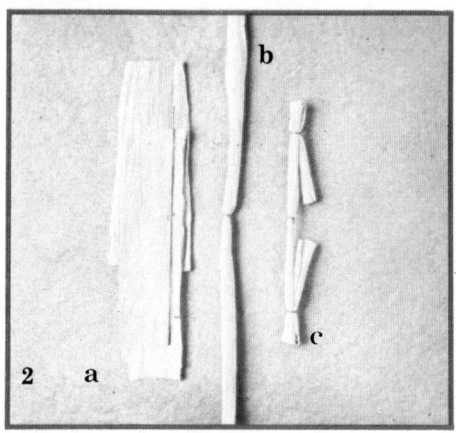

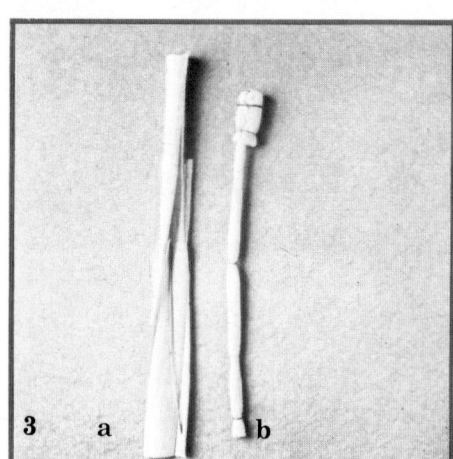

1. Making the body.
2. Assembling the arms.
3. Making the man's legs.

towel. Cut two 9cm (3½in) pieces of stem wire, one each for the body of each doll. Cut two 15cm (6in) pieces of stem wire for arms, one for each doll. Cut one 28cm (11in) piece of stem wire for man's legs. (Woman has skirt, so no legs are needed.) Cut about 20 pieces of thread, each 63cm (25in) long. Select two soaked shucks from the dish and gently blot them on towel.

Bodies Place one of the 9cm (3½in) wires lengthways on a shuck next to the edge (fig.1a). Fold top and bottom of shuck over ends of wire (fig.1b), then roll the wire up in the shuck. Using a piece of 63cm (25in) thread folded double, tie each end of the rolled shuck (fig.1c). To do this, place the middle of the double thread about 6mm (¼in) from the end of the rolled shuck, wrap around twice and tie in a double knot (this knot is used throughout). Trim off excess ends of thread. Do the same thing at the other end of the shuck. Repeat this process for the second body.

Arms Use two 15cm (6in) pieces of wire for the arms, one for each doll. Select four shucks. Try to ensure that they are of even length, width and colour, then the dolls' hands at the end of the arms will be identical. Using two shucks overlapped to extend the length to 20cm (8in), place one wire next to the edge of the overlapped shucks as for body, but this time without tucking in ends (fig.2c). Roll and tie centre tightly to hold wire and shucks (fig.2b).

Find the one end of the wire amid the rolled shuck and place your thumb on it. Gently bring the end of the shuck over the wire and tie about 18mm (¾in) from the end to make a loop for the hand. Repeat at the opposite end of the wire. Do not cut off extra shuck past the wrist as this helps to fill the sleeves (fig.2c). Repeat with the second 15cm (6in) piece of wire. Use the cocktail stick to open the loop without tearing the shuck.

Man's legs These are made from the 28cm (11in) wire. Use the same method as for bodies (see fig.1), since loops are not needed. Roll legs from three shucks which have been overlapped to make up the extra length of 32cm (13in) as shown in fig.3a. Tie at each end, 2.5cm (1in) from the end. Mark the middle with a knot of thread, so legs will be equal.

Shoes Use two shucks, one on top of the other, for each shoe. Fold both ends under towards the centre to make a piece 8cm (3in) wide. Roll the two pieces 4cm (1½in) onto the end of the made-up leg. Tie tightly at ankle and toe (fig.3b). Repeat for other shoe.

Heads These must be as round as possible. Fold thread double, ready to tie and knot. Select two shucks and lay one on top of the other, making double thickness. (If one shuck is used, it splits).

Select two extra shucks for filling. Holding one 9cm (3½in) rolled body, take the two filling shucks and tightly twist and wrap them around the top quarter of the body to make a ball (fig.4a).

Place the double shucks over the front of the body holding the covering shucks in place with your thumb. At the top of the 'head', give the covering shucks a full twist around (fig.4b) and bring them down behind the back of the head to produce a roundness. Tie twice with double thread tightly round neck below the ball and knot at the back (fig.4c). Make sure the front of the head is as smooth as possible. Do not cut off the extra shucks below the neck knot unless they cover the bottom knot on the body, as they will help fill the chest cavity. Repeat with other body piece.

Assembling and dressing Soak about 60 more shucks and cut more lengths of thread. Make sleeves first, assembling them on arms before attaching to doll. One set of arms will be for the woman's fancy sleeves, the other for the man.

Woman's sleeves Use eight shucks, four overlapping widths for each arm. With the widest part of the overlapping shucks towards the doll's hands, fold under the ends of the shucks about 2.5cm (1in) to meet at the centre of the arms. At the hand end of the arm, cut shuck edges with pinking shears (fig.5a). Roll all four shucks around arm, tie tightly at wrist and at centre arm (fig.5b). Make the other sleeve in exactly the same way.

Man's sleeves Use eight shucks and proceed as for woman's sleeves except that at the hand end of the arm, fold the shucks under just past the middle of hand for a hemmed look (fig.5c).

Trousers Use four overlapping shucks for each trouser leg. Measure shucks from just past centre of leg to top of shoes. Fold under at both ends to give hemmed look. Do not cover the top of the shoes as the foot will have to be bent later (fig.6). Tie tightly in centre and rather more loosely at cuff.

Woman's chest Lay sleeves horizontally across top of body, allowing a small space for the neck. Cut a 15cm (6in) piece of wire and, winding diagonally from waist to shoulder to waist again, wire arms to body securely (fig.7a). Fold one or more shucks in a 2.5cm (1in) square and lay it on the chest over the wire criss-cross.

Take four shucks, two doubled from the front and two doubled from the back, and criss-cross them over the square to hold it in place. Tie tightly with thread at the waist. (On both dolls, when you bring the shucks over the shoulder, push them into the neck to prevent a hunched appearance.) With pinking shears, cut two strips from a shuck and criss-cross these over the chest as a final touch for woman's blouse. Wrap thread around waist twice and tie. Make sure you can see the bottom body tie.

Man's body As for woman but leave out the folded square on the chest and use only four shucks to make the chest (fig.7b).

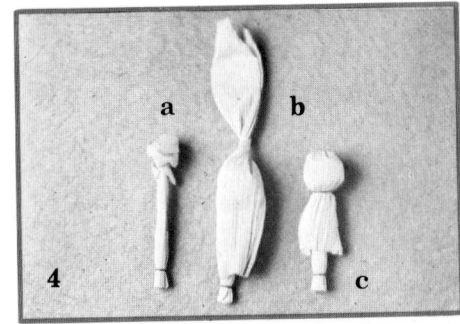

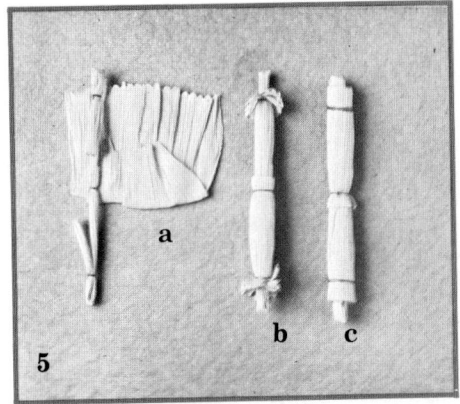

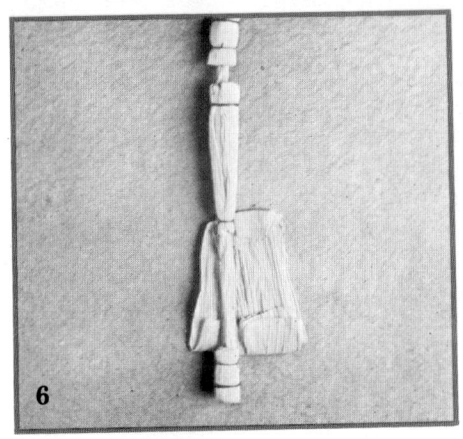

4. Shaping the head.
5. Sleeves for the arms.
6. Four shucks form a trouser leg.

Woman's skirt Either overlap shucks around bundles of rolled shucks to make a full skirt or, for a more economical method, wrap tissue paper around the centre body. Then apply about ten overlapping shucks to cover the tissue paper. Tie at the waist with thread, turn in the edges of the shucks at hemline and stuff with more tissue until dry. Tie three shucks together in a line and tie around bottom of skirt for decoration.

Man's legs If you are unable to see the bottom of the body knot, trim shucks. Find the centre of the legs and bend them in half. Make a wire hook and insert it into the bottom of the body at the knot. Bending each shoe at the ankle, lay legs on top of the hook on the body and press hook tightly onto legs.

Use five shucks, four to wrap around the legs, one for a good finish. Starting from the back, wrap between legs, around one leg and up around the waist. Repeat with second shuck on same leg, then do the same thing with two more shucks for the second leg. Fold the fifth shuck under top and bottom and fold in half again lengthways. Place it between the legs with neat edges showing.

Man's jacket Use eight shucks, four for the front and four for the back of the jacket. Spread out four overlapping shucks. Turn up about 18mm (¾in) at the bottom edge of the shucks. Lay the man on top of the shucks so that the folded edge is just below the split in his legs. At the back of his neck, separate the four shucks and bring them in pairs over the shoulders to the front. Pin all four where they cross at the centre of the chest with coloured pins.

Take the other four shucks, overlap them, fold under as for back shoulders just below the split in the legs and pin at the middle of the waistline. Take two pairs of shucks and turn at an angle from the top of the waist, pin to make lapels, then pull the pairs of shucks over the shoulders and pin down at the back. Trim off excess shucks at the back. Pin all shucks under the sides of the arms. Tie jacket in place with two shucks knotted together.

Hair Work clear-drying glue into a walnut-sized amount of corn silk until there is enough glue to hear it crunch between the fingers as you work it. Form it into a pancake and use fingers to mould the desired hair-style bringing in close to the head around the neck. For extra curls, roll a small amount of well-pasted corn silk in a matching colour and add that. Leave to dry.

Finishing Arrange the dolls' limbs into position while still wet and let the dolls dry for two weeks in an even temperature. Turn occasionally, so they dry thoroughly, inside and out.

When dolls are completely dry, paint on faces with acrylic or water-colour paints. Dolls can be preserved by spraying them when dry with inexpensive hair spray (this contains lacquer).

Above: Arms are wired to body. Below: A pair of delightful finished cornhusk dolls.

Glossary

Back-trac border A border put on after another, but going in the opposite direction.

Base The bottom of the basket.

Bodkin A sharp tool used for piercing. Also used for forming channels and splitting cane.

Border A decorative edge.

Bow The foundation of a handle.

Bye-stake A second stake which is inserted beside the main stake in order to strengthen.

Cane Material used in basketry. Available in various thicknesses, it is manufactured from rattan, a creeper from SE Asia which grows to enormous lengths.

Chain pair One round of pairing and one of reverse pairing. It is used to prevent oval work twisting.

Coil A shape used for decoration in rush work.

Corn dolly Derived from the word 'idol' and made from the last sheaf of the harvest, these were originally made as fertility symbols in a variety of shapes.

Cornshuckery A craft of the early American colonists who made dolls out of corn husks.

Clearer A tool such as a large nail which is used to clear holes in a seat which is being re-caned.

Close rand A method of randing which produces tight, closely woven work.

Diagonal weave A variation of pairing.

Five-straw favour A type of corn dolly made from five straws traditionally given by farm hands as love tokens.

Fitch A weave used after a space which grips the stakes firmly.

Follow-on border A border put on after another which goes in exactly the same direction.

Foot or footing Extra piece of work added onto the bottom of a basket.

Foot border Border added to the foot, or used on a basket with a wooden base.

Former Used in straw weaving as a core around which the weaving is shaped.

Herefordshire lantern A type of corn dolly.

Light randing Randing that is just touching – the opposite of close randing.

Mould Any conveniently shaped object which acts as the basic shape for baskets, hats etc in rush work.

Packing A weave used for shaping in basketry.

Pair, pairing A weave using two weavers, which is mostly used for making bases.

Piece in A method of joining in a new rod.

Plait [braid] border Decorative border, the true name is a vale border.

Randing Type of weave using only one weaver.

Rapping iron A tool used for levelling work, also used for close randing.

Reverse pairing A weave using two weavers which is the exact opposite of pairing, and counteracts twisting.

Rib randing A fancy weave using one weaver.

Rod border The most common type of border, often called a commercial border since it is the one most used by professional basket makers.

Round One complete round of work.

Round nosed pliers Tool used for nipping cane.

Screwblock A tool used in square work.

Shears A tool used for cutting.

Side cutters A tool used for cutting cane only.

Slype A method of pointing the ends of cane.

Stake Thick cane used for the framework.

Stake-up Process of inserting stakes into the base.

Step-up Stroke used to avoid a spiral look.

Suffolk horseshoe A type of corn dolly.

Trac border A decorative type of border.

Upsett A weave used to direct the shape of a basket from the base upwards.

Wale A weave using three or more weavers.

Weaver A single piece of cane or rush.

Index

Picture Credits
Steve Bicknell 24, 113
Roger Charity 64/5
Alan Duns 73, 75, 76, 96, 98, 98/9
Geoffrey Frosh 94, 100/1
Melvin Grey 21, 47, 87, 88/9, 90, 92, 103, 106
Peter Heinz 48/9, 53
Chris Holland 130
Louis Jordaan 74
Paul Kemp 8, 83, 84, 128
Chris Lewis 7
Dick Miller 16/17, 20, 22, 30, 33, 35, 39, 40, 50,
    62, 63, 66, 70
Alasdair Ogilvie 57
Johnnie Ryan 28/9
Kim Sayer 107, 125, 132
Transworld 78
Jerry Tubby 9, 34, 41, 61, 71, 119, 120
Rupert Watts 116, 127

Designers
Barbara Maynard 9, 21, 24, 28/9, 41, 57, 64/5,
    88/9, 94, 107
Anne Stone 125
Carolyn Tidmarsh 120

Artwork
Victoria Drew 11, 12, 13, 14, 15, 16, 18, 19
Barbara Maynard 23, 26, 31, 32, 36, 43, 44, 45,
    46, 51, 53, 54, 55, 56, 58, 59, 69, 70, 100/1
Coral Mula 122, 123, 124, 127, 128, 129
Linda Palmer 47
Kim Sayer 133, 134
Paul Williams 81, 82, 84, 87, 91, 96, 97, 103,
    104, 105, 109, 112, 114, 115